STUDENT DRAMA SERIES

General Editor: MICHAEL MARLAND, B.A.

THEATRE
CHOICE

THEATRE CHOICE

A COLLECTION OF MODERN SHORT PLAYS

COMPILED *BY* MICHAEL MARLAND, B.A.

HEADMASTER
WOODBERRY DOWN SCHOOL
LONDON

BLACKIE *LONDON & GLASGOW*

Blackie & Son Limited
BISHOPBRIGGS, GLASGOW
5 FITZHARDINGE STREET
PORTMAN SQUARE
LONDON, W.1

This collection of plays,
Introduction and Notes   ©   *Michael Marland, 1972*
The Wake   ©   *Alun Owen, 1972*
Double, Double   ©   *James Saunders, 1964*
No Why   ©   *John Whiting, 1961*
See the Pretty Lights   ©   *Alan Plater, 1972*
Last Day in Dreamland   ©   *Willis Hall, 1960*

FIRST PUBLISHED 1972
ISBN 0 216 87641 9

PRINTED IN GREAT BRITAIN BY
WESTERN PRINTING SERVICES LTD, BRISTOL

 CONTENTS

ACKNOWLEDGMENTS

The compiler is grateful to the authors and their agents for their help in the preparation of this volume:

Felix de Wolfe & Associates for *The Wake* by Alun Owen.
Margaret Ramsay for *Double, Double* by James Saunders and *See the Pretty Lights* by Alan Plater.
A. D. Peters & Co. for *No Why* by John Whiting.
Harvey Unna Ltd. for *Last Day in Dreamland* by Willis Hall from *A Glimpse of the Sea*.

INTRODUCTION

There's no doubt about it: the theatre developed a new excitement in the second half of the fifties. For many it had always been an especially vivid experience of living, but also it was usually cocooned by matinee teas and plush, by polite characters and French windows, by upper-middle-class life and genteel language—no wonder, then, that most of the major theatrical excitements of the immediate post war days were revivals of the classics. But in the mid-fifties there was a change: the Royal Court and John Osborne's *Look Back in Anger* (1956); the visit of Brecht[1] with his German actors in the Berliner Ensemble (1956); the impact of French writers such as Samuel Beckett (*Waiting for Godot*, 1955) and Ionesco (*The Lesson*, 1955); the discovery of 'working-class' writers and backgrounds (Wesker's *Chicken Soup With Barley*, 1958); especially with Joan Littlewood's east end Theatre Workshop (1956). All this was confirmed and amplified by a stimulating and experimental output of plays on sound radio (especially the Third Programme), and soon the creation of virtually a new school of television playwrights.

One critic (Irving Wardle of *The Times*) has summed up these huge changes by saying that 'the theatre re-established contact with society'.[2] There was a feeling that the theatre was opening up. 'Glamour' was being replaced by *concern*; the West End by the whole country; and the range of subjects, atmospheres, feelings, and ways of creating 'a play' were hugely extended. Not all the highest hopes of the heady excitement of the late fifties have developed successfully, but still the British theatre today has more to say, in a wider variety of forms, and to a wider variety of audiences than ever. It is significant that during this time drama in schools and for examinations has flourished as never before, and that even examiners (especially in CSE) have widened their earlier range of drama.

No one volume can hope to span the period, especially as not all the dramatists have written many shorter plays (e.g. John Osborne), and, anyway, some plays are already available to

[1] See, for instance, the edition of *The Caucasian Chalk Circle* in this series.
[2] Introduction to *Theatre at Work*, Methuen, 1967, p. 16.

schools. However the five plays in this collection do represent a fair sample of the new British drama and its authors, as well as of the modes of writing from the romantic naturalism of *The Wake* to the zany hysteria of *Double, Double*. Students wanting to extend their reading can move onto the list on page 189, together with the recommended plays in the notes on the authors.

However, the plays have been chosen less as 'examples' than as strong dramatic experiences in themselves—likely to make an impact on the student reader or actor. Even the enigmatic *No Why* by John Whiting has an inescapable power, and the horrific effect of the conventionally perfect happy family on the wretched boy has a disturbing relevance to many moments of life.

I have been particularly anxious to make sure that the pieces chosen do justice to their authors, and are not by ill chance their weaker plays. In fact each of these, whatever its weight, is, I am convinced, a good example of its author's work. Thus the critic John Russell Taylor has said of *Double, Double*: 'slight but persuasive, it is one of the best things Saunders has ever done'. *The Wake* seems to me a good example of Alun Owen's easy naturalism and exploration of family and local tensions. Willis Hall's *Last Day in Dreamland* is surely far superior to many of his later full-length plays, and although Alan Plater's humorous non-romance in *See the Pretty Lights* is again light weight, its delicacy and sympathetic balance, together with the real humour of the dialogue, make it an outstanding example of his subtle writing. A noticeable characteristic of each play is that it achieves a balance between ambition and achievement; none of the plays sets out to explore more than is possible in its compass: there is a depth, but no strain.

It is no accident that the first play in a collection called *Theatre Choice* should in fact be in the form of a television script. For earlier generations the novel and short story were the main literary forms, and it was to these prose narratives that the theatre most closely related. It is not surprising that two of the plays in the earlier volume in the series, *Spotlight* (Conrad's *One Day More* and Pirandello's *Limes from Sicily*), were adapted by the authors from their own short stories. Today, though, television is arguably the dominant medium, and there is a very close relationship between radio plays (see *Worth a Hearing* in this series), television plays, and the stage itself. Alun Owen, for instance, sees no distinction between the media, having declared: 'I write plays. If they are in two or three acts they are stage plays: if they are in one act they are television plays, because what else can one do with a one-act play?' In fact, of course, his play here could easily be staged in a hall, especially perhaps an open stage. Of the others, only *No Why* was conceived unambiguously for 'the stage'. *See the Pretty Lights* has been heard as a radio play; *Last Day in Dreamland* started as a television play; and *Double, Double,* printed here as a stage play, has been seen on television as *Just You Wait,* and heard on the radio as plain *Gimlet*!

'Drama' is in many ways a misleading word: there's little 'dramatic' in the everyday sense in these plays. Nothing happens to Norman and Enid in *See the Pretty Lights*—that is the point; the possible punch-up in *The Wake* is actually avoided. Even the death in *No Why* is at the very end—after the action is over. Nevertheless for reading or for acting these five plays will be found humorous and moving explorations of experience, pushing across the frontiers of naturalism. They are, in their different modes, indeed compelling pieces of dramatic imagination.

MICHAEL MARLAND

The Wake

by Alun Owen

The action takes place in a small working-class house in Liverpool, and the compartment of a train.

CHARACTERS

TERRY O'NEILL ⎫
JOEY O'NEILL ⎬ three brothers
BILLY O'NEILL ⎭

HETTIE MAGEE

JUDY, who lives with Terry

ACTING NOTE

No public performances of this play may be given without prior permission. All requests for performing rights (both amateur and professional) should be directed to:
Felix de Wolfe & Associates,
61 Berkeley House,
15 Hay Hill,
London W1X 7LH

✳ ✳ ✳
The Wake

SCENE I   A FIRST CLASS CARRIAGE IN A TRAIN

Night

TERRY *and* JUDY *are sitting opposite each other in the corner seats by the window. The time is late afternoon/early evening; season, winter.*

TERRY *is thirty and handsome after the Irish manner (i.e. slightly florid). He will run to fat. He is well dressed and has only the slightest trace of a Liverpool inflexion.*

JUDY *is twenty-one, very pretty and bright. She is bored with* Nova *magazine, but* TERRY *is absorbed in the* New Statesman. *There is a constant tension between them,* TERRY *repulsing her natural enthusiasm. A thought strikes* JUDY.

1   JUDY. Hey! Should I be wearing black?

2   TERRY. What?

3   JUDY. Should I be wearing black?

4   TERRY. Oh, for God's sake!

5   JUDY. Well, should I?

6   TERRY. Why?

7   JUDY. It's usual, isn't it?

8   TERRY. Don't you know?

9   JUDY. Would I be asking if I knew? No one's ever died in my family.

10 TERRY [*wearily*]. If you examine that remark, you'll . . . [*He interrupts himself impatiently.*] Anyway, if I thought you should be in black I'd have let you know smartish.

11 JUDY. Then it's all right?

12 TERRY. Yes, it's all right.

> *There is a pause while* JUDY *thinks. When she speaks it is as if she is answering a question.*

13 JUDY. Yes but in a way, it seems pointless going now.

14 TERRY [*sighing*]. You're determined, aren't you?

3

1 JUDY. Determined what?

2 TERRY. Not to let me read the John Morgan article.

3 JUDY [snorting]. Phuhh, you hate John Morgan's stuff, you're always saying you don't know why you read his stuff.

4 TERRY. I like to keep my eye on him just to make sure he's running true to form.

5 JUDY. I like him.

6 TERRY. You would. And why is it pointless going now?

7 JUDY. Oh well, I don't mean this the way it'll sound . . . but isn't it too late.

8 TERRY. I'm his son.

9 JUDY. Yes, I suppose so, but it's a pity you didn't go before. [TERRY gives her a cold look.] What'll I do?

10 TERRY. I've told you, wait at the hotel.

11 JUDY. I can't come to the house, can I?

12 TERRY. No, you can't . . . I'm sorry, love, but it's better to let me go there first. I'll probably have to see the Priest and all that.

13 JUDY. I can't imagine you with a priest.

14 TERRY. Oh, I'm great. I snap into a cringe with a Catholic layman's reflex that you'd never know from the real thing.

15 JUDY. Wouldn't I?

16 TERRY [smiling at her]. No, love, you wouldn't. It's better you don't come to the house; you don't know them; you can't begin to understand what it's like. How could you? It's another country and you don't know the tribal customs. That's why I didn't want you to come in the first place.

17 JUDY. But I wanted to come.

18 TERRY [avoiding her eyes and looking out of the window]. I don't really believe it yet, you know.

19 JUDY. He was a nice man.

20 TERRY [flatly]. Yeah, a nice man.

4

1 JUDY. Have I said the wrong thing?

2 TERRY. It's very difficult to say the right thing, whatever that may be.

3 JUDY. I didn't really know him.

4 TERRY [*wryly*]. You didn't have much chance.

5 JUDY. Who'll be there?

6 TERRY. I don't know—well, Hettie, she'll be there of course.

7 JUDY. Of course . . . how old is Hettie?

8 TERRY. Fiftyish—that's a funny question.

9 JUDY. Why? I just wondered.

10 TERRY. But I thought you knew.

11 JUDY. How would I? You never mentioned it and she's not a relative.

12 TERRY. No. Funny, I just took it for granted you knew all about her.

13 JUDY. Maybe one of your brothers'll be there.

14 TERRY. Can't see that; Billy's at sea, and the man's not been in the house in years.

15 JUDY. I never heard you call Joey that before.

16 TERRY. What?

17 JUDY. You called him 'the man'.

18 TERRY. We always called him that. The old man called it him first and it stuck.

19 JUDY. Why?

20 TERRY. I haven't spoken to Joey—I mean properly spoken to him in years. We were never the same sort and . . .

21 JUDY [*cutting in*]. No, I meant why did your father call him 'the man'?

22 TERRY. Well he—d'you know, I can't remember. I mean, he just did. I suppose there was a reason. The old fella wasn't given to nicknames. [*definitely*] No, I can't remember and it really doesn't matter. [*He resumes his reading.*]

1 JUDY. Is it easy?

2 TERRY [*patiently*]. Is what easy?

3 JUDY. Making the arrangements for the thingy?

4 TERRY. The thingy? Oh, for god's sake, Judy, it's a funeral.

5 JUDY. Yes, but I . . .

6 TERRY. Isn't it marvellous? You're afraid of saying it, aren't you? The next thing you'll be spelling it: Terry's father D.I.E.D.'d.

7 JUDY [*hurt*]. Well, I'm sorry. I just don't know what you do when these things happen.

8 TERRY. He died of natural causes. There's a death certificate. The Priest'll take over that side and I'll go to the under-taker.

9 JUDY. Undertaker?

10 TERRY. Yeah, he's a pretty important guy on these occasions. It's not difficult. It's embarrassing but not difficult.

11 JUDY. Is there a will?

12 TERRY. I don't know. I suppose so but he wouldn't have that much: insurance, the house, few hundred.

13 JUDY. You're bloody calm.

14 TERRY. If you mean cold, say so.

15 JUDY. All right cold.

16 TERRY. I told you not to come.

17 JUDY. I hoped you might have needed me.

18 TERRY. Thanks.

19 JUDY. I should have known better.

20 TERRY. I'm very upset, you know.

21 JUDY [*coldly*]. Are you?

22 TERRY. You'll have to take my word.

23 JUDY. Were you frightened of him?

24 TERRY. Joey?

25 JUDY. Who?

1   TERRY [*covering up*]. Oh, you mean the Daddy. Of course not. We were different, but I respected him.

2   JUDY. He thought you were a hellova big gun.

3   TERRY. Well, I only gave him a couple of worries.

4   JUDY [*smiling*]. What was the other one?

5   TERRY. I had a bout of religious mania when I was fourteen. The old fella's a fair enough catholic but when pushed he confesses to being anti-clerical. [JUDY *looks blank*.] He hadn't much time for priests. Anyway, he didn't have much to worry about. I think you'll agree I'm a committed womaniser.

6   JUDY. Well, I'll agree that's how you see yourself.

    TERRY *throws down his magazine*.

7   TERRY. When you've read the same line seven times I think you should call it a day. . . . Why all the questions tonight?

8   JUDY. What do you know about me?

9   TERRY [*rapidly*]. You? Oh, you were born in Kensington, only child, Dad's a doctor, Mum's a Mum, they love you, you love them and you went to the Lycée. You've got four male cousins and two female with an assortment of upper-middle aunties and uncles to go with 'em. You spent your summers in Provence, but for some obscure reason never went to the winter sports. All right?

10   JUDY. It sounds a bit bleak but all right.

11   TERRY. It sounds pretty cosy to me.

12   JUDY. Do you know what I know about you?

13   TERRY. All right, work me a breakdown.

14   JUDY. Terence O'Neill, thirty, *married,* executive, one of three brothers: Joey, Billy, Terry. Father, docker; Mother, dead. Father nice little man, blue eyes, voice like gravel, broken fingernails but he's dead now . . . you must admit I'm a little short on the white meat.

15   TERRY [*drily*]. Terry O'Neill, left home at eighteen, separated from his brothers by Oxford, separated from his father

by qualifications. Jumped the class line, left his wife, co-habits with a girl called Judy. Talks posh now and regrets it only when he's had three too many, when Liverpool won the cup, or when Everton had the league.

2 JUDY. I wish you'd have a drink now.

3 TERRY. Time enough at the Wake. [*He looks out of the window.*] I wish I'd driven up. [*He looks around the compartment.*] This is just a place, a shaking place that'll arrive and the black outside doesn't give me anything—just black, no image, no sense of going uphill to the North—nothing but black.

4 JUDY. Will she be there—you're wife?

5 TERRY. Shouldn't think so. Don't care anyway.

TERRY *closes his eyes and croons to himself.*

They asked me my country,
I told 'em my name,
I'll tell 'em my name again and again.
'Cos me father and mother were both Kerrymen.

6 JUDY. What's that?

7 TERRY. Something my old Paddy Daddy used to sing when he was at a loss for words. He used it to buy himself time, till he'd made up his mind, decided his next move.

8 JUDY. Will there be any more there—relatives, friends, you know?

9 TERRY. There might be—well, not relatives—there aren't any—he'd got the odd mate though.

10 JUDY. How'll your brothers take it?

11 TERRY. Billy'll cry, sob a lot. He's like a woman, he can still cry. You know how they say, 'You'll feel better after a good cry, dear'. Well, that's our Billy. He'll cry, then he'll cheer up. He'll probably have three rounds of tears before and during the funeral. After that he'll be manly and reliable. He's not very complicated.

12 JUDY [*fascinated by his lack of passion*]. And Joey?

1   TERRY [*flippantly*]. Joey? I don't know and really I have no machinery for dealing with questions about Joey. I've no interest in him so I prefer not to speculate.

2   JUDY. They're your brothers, Terry.

3   TERRY. And my father's dead. Does that mean we have to play Happy Families all the way to Liverpool?

4   JUDY. No, I just wondered. I can't help it.

TERRY *leans forward and with complete passion lets his next speech pour out of him without reserve.*

5   TERRY. All right! I hate the sight of our Joey, I always did and I always will. Our Joey's big, strong, dishonest, violent, cruel, charming. You name the worst excesses of the Irish character, leaving out all the virtues, and you've got Joey. He's a thief, a liar, clever, quick. He can hurt you and he does. He had a procession of policemen at our house for as long as I can remember. My old fella was as straight as that one's cork-screwed. The day I was presented with a book by the Lord Mayor our Joey was in Court Three, Juvenile Division. Straight out of the Mayor's parlour we went, round to Dale Street, with my book in my hand. It felt as if I was carrying a piece of filth not *A Golden Treasury of English Verse* bound in hand-tooled leather. So don't ask me about our Joey. I tried never to think about him but whenever I was with the old man that damned thing sat between us. So I couldn't explain to my father. I couldn't put him right, tell him how it was with me, make him understand. I wanted to, yeah, I wanted. There was no one else I wanted to give my side of it to. I don't believe in excuses—what you do—that's it mostly, but I wouldn't have minded telling the Dad—only not with our Joey sitting grinning his sly grin, and giving the unbelieving nudge. He always dirtied everything. Can you see a ten-year-old with big blue eyes, black curly hair and a leer of cynical disbelief all over his face? Well, that was our Joey. So don't ask me how he'll take it, 'cos he is wicked enough to be different just to spite me. [*He falls back, spent.*]

1   JUDY. I'm sorry. I didn't know you were so hard-pressed, baby.

SCENE 2   THE O'NEILL'S HOUSE

That night

The O'Neill house is tiny, two up and two down, with a scullery beyond. You step into the living room straight from the street. There is no hallway. The stairs mount steeply up against the wall to the rooms above. The room is over-furnished making movement difficult.

HETTIE MAGEE *is sitting alone. She is a working-class, Liverpool Irish woman, outspoken and sour from hard work.*

BILLY O'NEILL *enters the front door and is right into the room.* BILLY *is a nondescript man. He looks older than* TERRY *but he is doomed to age quickly. He is weak in the presence of death and* HETTIE—*a formidable combination. He is always anxious to please.* HETTIE *treats him like a child.*

2   HETTIE [*sighing*]. Will you eat something, Billy?

3   BILLY. Should I?

4   HETTIE. It's up to you, son . . . will you eat?

5   BILLY. Yeah, I suppose I should.

6   HETTIE [*patiently*]. What'll you have like? What'll I make you?

7   BILLY. Oh, anything.

8   HETTIE. I'll give you a fry, a bit of bacon and fried cabbage like.

9   BILLY [*brightens*]. That'd be great. [*He remembers.*] I mean, thanks very much.

HETTIE *rises to go.*

10   HETTIE [*to herself*]. And I sent off that telegram hours ago.

11   BILLY [*glad to agree*]. Aye, you did.

12   HETTIE. You'd think he'd have replied.

13   BILLY. Oh, he'll be on his way. He'd have dropped everything like, when he got it, and be on his way.

14   HETTIE. Aye, you're right, on his way.

1   BILLY. Did you do anything about Joey?

2   HETTIE. I sent Alan Hogan's lad out to tell him.

3   BILLY. And he'd know where to . . . [*He trails off.*]

4   HETTIE [*cutting in*]. Oh, he'd know. He's been in trouble himself. He'd know all right, know where to look, know his area sort of thing. Did you get a bottle when you were below?

5   BILLY. They won't serve a full bottle. Seemingly it's not their policy so I got two halves. [*He produces two half bottles from his coat pockets.*] Will we have one? Is it all right like?

6   HETTIE. Oh, aye. I'll get the glasses.

She takes a couple of glasses from the sideboard as BILLY *opens the bottle.* BILLY *pours them each a good drink.*

He was a good man.

BILLY *starts to cry.*

Get that malt down you, son; it'll stop the salt.

BILLY *obediently drinks with a gulp and stops crying.*

7   BILLY. I don't want a fry, just a piece of bread and butter.

8   HETTIE. I've some butter in the scullery.

She goes out to get it while BILLY *mooches around the room, unconsciously humming the same tune as* TERRY *sang earlier.* HETTIE *comes back with the bread.*

9   BILLY. It was lucky like, me bein' home.

10   HETTIE. Lucky?

11   BILLY. Well, I mean, I'm glad I was home and not at sea.

12   HETTIE. Aye, I suppose at least he had one of you'se by him, the runt of the litter but one of you'se. [*She sighs.*] Oh, Pat, you were a grand chap and the brewery'll miss you, but you were entitled. You punished yourself with workin'. [*She turns on* BILLY.] And he was a good Da' to you lot.

13   BILLY [*uncomfortable*]. Oh, he was first . . . as a dad like.

1 HETTIE. And none of you appreciated him.

2 BILLY. We did.

3 HETTIE [*scornfully*]. Call yourselves sons . . . I've seen better flat irons.

4 BILLY. I'm here, aren't I?

5 HETTIE [*bitterly*]. Aye, you're here, God help you. I can't walk up the street; they're waitin' for me, the women. 'Are his lads there?' and all I can face 'em with is, 'Billy's home'.

6 BILLY. Well, that's not my fault and I'm here. I could have been in India or somethin', couldn't I?

7 HETTIE [*tartly*]. India'd be a better story. And that Joey's paradin' the town, in and out of the shebeens,* the clubs, better he was in Walton.

8 BILLY [*indignantly*]. I don't see that. Honest to God. I don't see how you make that one out.

9 HETTIE [*scornfully*]. 'One fella's out in India, the other's captured, and I'm waitin' on the college one', and you can't see that as a story? God help you, Billy, you were always a slowcoach.

10 BILLY. Ah, that's just a lot of women's talk for the doorstep, just woman's talk.

11 HETTIE. What do you think I am, a buck navvy, you soft head, you!

12 BILLY. Look, I'm here and I'm not answering for the rest of our lot. Oh, it was always the same in this house. 'Our Terry's doin' his homework. Shurrup!' 'Where's our Joey, what's he done now? Shurrup!' I never gave no one trouble and I'm here. Where are they? Go on, where are the sharpies? Scattered, aren't they? But Billy's here so give him a hard time. He's only Billy!

13 HETTIE. Shurrup, and be a man!

14 BILLY [*rounding on her*]. What's that mean? Batter somebody or run off with a girl 'cos that's all them fellers were good for! Ah, you make me sick!

* illegal drinking clubs.

1 HETTIE [*sighing*]. Yeah, Billy, you were always the good one.

2 BILLY [*continuing*]. Yeah, I was always the good one and he knew it in the end. I did all right by him. You lot might not know it but he did. I'm a bosun and it's good money. I've been with the same company for ten years. I may not be a scholar but I'm a good bosun.

3 HETTIE [*indifferently*]. I'm sorry, lad.

4 BILLY. I'll believe you. Thousands wouldn't.

5 HETTIE. Oh, if you're going to go mardy* on us.

6 BILLY. You'd better get this right, Hettie. I've got men who do what I tell 'em. I may be spare here but I'm a gaffer on sea.

7 HETTIE. All right! I've said I'm sorry. I'm not going to clean your boots.

8 BILLY [*doggedly*]. Just so we understand each other, that's all.

9 HETTIE [*quietly*]. Oh, I understand you all right, Billy, you may be able to order around a few lascar sailors and kid that company of yours but this is Hettie Magee your talkin' to. I've changed you when you wet your pants. I stopped 'em thumpin' you and I know why you ran off to sea. I understand you, Billy, like you were one of me own.

   BILLY *is about to answer angrily, but there is a knock at the door.*

   It'll be somebody.

10 BILLY [*doubtfully*]. Will you go?

   But HETTIE *has already pushed past him to open the door.*
   TERRY, *now wearing an overcoat, steps into the room.*

11 HETTIE. Well, at least you came.

12 TERRY. I'd every intention of coming. I left as soon as I got the telegram.

13 HETTIE. Will you eat somethin'?

* behaving like a spoilt child.

1   TERRY [*smiling*]. Hello, Billy.

2   BILLY. Hello.

3   HETTIE. A cup of tea and a sandwich?

4   TERRY. You were home when it happened then.

5   BILLY. Yeah.

6   HETTIE. But I sent the telegram.

    TERRY *turns to her before speaking.*

7   TERRY. I know.

8   BILLY. I've been home a week.

9   TERRY. I'm glad one of us was here.

10   HETTIE. He wouldn't let me send for you, I wanted to but . . .

11   TERRY [*cutting her off*]. Billy was here.

12   BILLY. Yeah, I was here. Will you have a drink?

13   TERRY. Sure, what have you got?

14   HETTIE. There's only whisky. You'll take what we've got.

15   TERRY [*mildly*]. Of course. Where is he?

16   HETTIE. In the front bedroom.

17   TERRY. Has the Priest been?

18   HETTIE. I don't know how you can ask!

19   TERRY [*coldly*]. Hettie, I'm here because my father, who I loved, is dead, not to have you read me a lecture on my personal morality.

20   HETTIE. Words, words, that was all you were ever good at. You're a talker, son.

21   TERRY. I can be very silent and if you're going to carry on like that I'm not even stopping.

    Before HETTIE *can speak he stops her.*

No! Just for a change try listening and letting this get through. I am not a little boy for you to abuse and shout at and if I have a single difficult moment, I shall go, do you understand me, have I made myself quite clear?

14

1 HETTIE. You can't talk . . .

2 TERRY. Oh yes I can, it's my father who is dead. Well, I'm not here to give *you* an emotional holiday. That's all I have to say. All right.?

HETTIE is furious but impotent.

3 HETTIE. All right, Mister, and I've done with you'se!

4 TERRY. Can I count on that? [*He turns to* BILLY.] I'll have that drink if I may, Billy.

BILLY is flabbergasted by HETTIE's *rout. He speaks without thinking.*

5 BILLY. Yes, sir—I mean . . .

HETTIE gives BILLY *a scornful look and* BILLY, *shamefacedly, pours* TERRY *a drink.*

Here you are, our kid.

6 TERRY. Thanks, hadn't you better give Hettie one?

7 BILLY. Oh aye, sure.

8 HETTIE. No. Are you stoppin' here?

9 TERRY. We're at a hotel.

10 HETTIE. You're not bringin' that girl in . . .

11 TERRY [*over her*]. She's not here, is she? Anyway, I never stay here, you know that. When did it happen?

12 BILLY. About three this mornin'.

13 HETTIE. He dozed off.

14 BILLY. Aye, he dozed off. He never came back like, very peaceful, you know.

15 TERRY. I'm glad. Have the arrangements been made?

16 HETTIE. I sent a message to the undertakers. It'll be tomorrow, are you stoppin'?

17 TERRY. Yes. Is there a will?

18 HETTIE. The fella's comin' about it in the mornin'. I'll leave you two to talk. I'll wash them dishes while you talk.

She goes out.

1   TERRY. That's better. How goes it, Billy?

2   BILLY [*brightening*]. Oh, not so bad, I think I'm goin' to Aussie next trip.

3   TERRY. You'll like that.

4   BILLY [*touchily*]. You been, have you?

5   TERRY. No.

6   BILLY. Well, how'd you know I'd like it?

7   TERRY. I don't. I just thought you might.

8   BILLY [*sulkily*]. Aye, I suppose so.

9   TERRY. If he's left the house to us, you can have my share.

10   BILLY. We'll wait and see first before you start gettin' generous.

11   TERRY [*sighing*]. As you wish, did anyone get in touch with Joey?

12   BILLY. She's sent a lad to look for him.

13   TERRY. Good.

14   BILLY. You've brought the girl with you then?

15   TERRY. She wanted to come.

16   BILLY. She's a young bit, isn't she?

17   TERRY. Twenty-one.

18   BILLY. Oh aye, I saw your lad on Tuesday.

19   TERRY. Yes?

20   BILLY. Nice-lookin' kid. He came round to see if Hettie needed any messages.

21   TERRY. By himself? Came round here by himself? What's that woman thinking of?

22   BILLY. He's five. I did messages when I was five. You may not have but . . .

23   TERRY [*cutting in*]. Yes, I know, only . . .

24   BILLY [*ploughing on*]. Don't tell us, this is different, he's your lad not just Billy.

25   TERRY. I never said that, I just don't think children of five should be running around the streets on their own. . . .

You seem very edgy tonight, picking me up on every
word.

2   BILLY. Well, things have changed. The daddy's not comin'
down them stairs and hushin' me 'cos the college
puddin's home. Things have changed.

3   TERRY. Billy, I'm not here to quarrel with you. We're both
here for the same reason, he was our father.

4   BILLY. I stay in the house. I do the right thing.

5   TERRY. You always did. It's your nature. You're a good man,
Billy.

6   BILLY. And he knew it.

7   TERRY. Of course he did.

8   BILLY. He never had to worry over me.

9   TERRY [slightly irritated]. He used to stay with me in London.

10 BILLY. Only 'cos you wouldn't come here. We weren't good
enough for you.

11 TERRY. Look, if you're going to behave like Hettie I don't
need it. You can't have a monopoly of grief. After all,
you're only here by accident. I came, despite everything
you'd like to say. I came and when we've buried him
I'm going back. We've got different worlds you and I,
Billy. We don't have to see each other any more after
this, but let's try and behave like grown-up men now.

12 BILLY. All right but for his sake.

13 TERRY. No, for our sakes. It's not an easy time. Why make it
worse?

14 BILLY. She's right. You're a talker. You always were.

    TERRY loses his patience.

15 TERRY. Yes, I'm a talker that declares six grand and finds a
way round four more. How much do you take home,
Billy? [He has expended his anger.] Oh, what's the use, you
don't like me and I don't really mind. All I ask for is a
truce. Is it on?

16 BILLY. Aye, I suppose so . . .

17

He offers his hand to TERRY. TERRY *is surprised at this childish gesture. For a moment he stares at the outstretched hand, then with a rueful smile he takes it.*

Do you really earn that much, our kid?

2 TERRY. What? [*He smiles.*] Oh yeah, but don't tell the Collector, he's got a tapeworm that's only greedy for my money.

There is a thundering knock at the outside door that makes both BILLY *and* TERRY *jump to their feet. As they cross to the door* HETTIE *comes in from the kitchen.*
BILLY *opens the door and a man pushes past him. It is* JOEY O'NEILL. *He is a vigorous man—attractive, dark-haired, curly and blue-eyed. He is dressed beautifully but the animal vigour of the man is the most striking thing about him. He is violent and very ready. He crosses to* HETTIE *ignoring his brothers. He is quietly furious.*

3 JOEY. Listen you—you don't send scruffs lookin' for Joey. God, I ought to cripple you! Me father's dead and I have to hear it from a no-mark like Alan Hogan's melt.

4 HETTIE [*boldly*]. I sent one of your own kidney.

JOEY *manages to control himself.*

5 JOEY. Where is he?
6 TERRY. Now, Joey.
7 JOEY. Cut out, you! [*to* HETTIE] I'm waitin', where is he?
8 HETTIE. The front bedroom.
9 BILLY [*moving in*]. Will you have a . . .

JOEY'S *look silences* BILLY, *who backs off.*

10 JOEY [*to* TERRY]. Have *you* seen him?
11 TERRY. No, I've just arrived.
12 JOEY. Why aren't you up there then?
13 TERRY. I . . .
14 JOEY. Move.
15 TERRY. Well . . .
16 JOEY [*barking*]. Move!

TERRY *crosses to the staircase and follows* JOEY *upstairs.*

SCENE 3 THE O'NEILL'S HOUSE

Later in the evening

HETTIE *is seated looking at the staircase and* BILLY *is pacing the room.*

1 HETTIE. Have you got worms or somethin'? Sit down.

2 BILLY. I'm waitin' on 'em.

TERRY *and* JOEY *come downstairs.* TERRY *is first, both are dry-eyed.*

3 TERRY. I didn't realize that he was so frail.

4 BILLY. Y'what?

5 JOEY. He said frail. That's what he said. Your old fella looks frail.

6 BILLY. Oh.

JOEY *helps himself to a drink.*

7 JOEY. You didn't cross yourself.

8 TERRY. Didn't I?

9 JOEY. Hadn't got the guts for it, had you or don't they go in for respect where you come from?

10 TERRY [*turning away*]. What sort of a question's that?

11 BILLY [*to* JOEY]. Leave him alone.

12 JOEY [*coldly*]. Don't you get brave with me, son, or I'll mark you. How long you been home?

13 BILLY. Came last week.

14 JOEY. You're me brother and you didn't come and find me.

15 BILLY [*weakly*]. He wouldn't let me.

16 JOEY. Y'what?

17 HETTIE. He's giving it to you straight. He didn't want you worried. Any road it had been left too long.

18 JOEY [*indicating* TERRY]. How'd the queer fella there get up so quickly?

19 TERRY. They sent me a telegram.

1 JOEY. But I had to be served notice by a detention-centre drop-out. He was my Daddy too, you know!

2 TERRY. Of course he was and if things haven't been done in quite the right way, we're all sorry but death isn't tidy, you know.

3 JOEY [*dismissing him*]. If you're goin' to talk like a milk-leg, better you say nothin', son. [*to* HETTIE] I fixed an undertaker.

4 HETTIE. I got one.

5 JOEY. Mine's better.

6 HETTIE. I've already . . .

7 JOEY. Mine's the best! [*He turns on* TERRY *and grins.*] So, the Hero's come home, has he?

8 HETTIE. He brought that girl with him.

9 JOEY [*coldly*]. What's that to do with you?

10 HETTIE. It's a livin' sin . . .

11 JOEY. And he'll burn. You don't play any new ones, do you? You can go.

HETTIE *is about to reply but thinks better of it and goes.*

[*to* TERRY] I want you out of this town straight after the funeral.

12 TERRY. I beg your pardon?

13 JOEY. You heard, at the funeral but then out, understood?

14 TERRY. Look, Joey, I don't know who you think you're talking to, but . . .

15 JOEY. I know just who I'm talkin' to.

16 TERRY. Never the less, don't try giving me orders.

17 JOEY [*quietly*]. No?

18 BILLY. Shurrup, our Terry. He means it. He'll duff you if you cross him.

19 JOEY. You'd do well to listen to your brother. He may not be much but he's got all his beans and if you're within

20

twenty miles of Windsor street the day after tomorrow, you'll hurt all over.

> TERRY *moves towards* JOEY.

2 TERRY. Now look here.

> *Very rapidly* JOEY *slaps him with an open hand on either cheek and finishes up with a token chop on his arm. There is no pain in the blows only humiliation.*

3 JOEY. And they were just love taps. [*He laughs.*] No, get back to your hotel and your skirt. I'll send for you when your needed.

4 TERRY. He was my father.

5 JOEY. So you'll be there. I need the dressin'. You, Billy and Hettie?

6 BILLY. And you?

7 JOEY. Have your brains gone soft? The old fella was a decent man and even if he did have three wash-outs for sons they'll be there. Billy, you'll have this fella's lad with you.

8 TERRY. Is that necessary?

9 JOEY. It's proper and this is goin' to be done proper, everythin' right. . . . The livin' are goin' to be tidy.

10 TERRY [*ironically*]. You're taking over, aren't you, Joey?

11 JOEY. And why wouldn't I?

12 BILLY [*agreeing*]. Yeah, he's the eldest.

13 TERRY. And that's reason enough?

14 JOEY. You've no case—I'm eldest.

15 TERRY. I could give you a very good case. I'm no wash-out. I'm a success. I've a good job and better prospects and whether you like it or not, father was proud of me. I never heard him boast about you.

16 JOEY. He never did but I never shamed him.

17 TERRY. And you believe that?

18 JOEY. You mean me record? Oh, any family can have one of my sort, we grow 'em around here instead of Michaelmas

Daisies. Mind, we've always been a bit short on fellas who walk out on girls.

2 TERRY. I've always supported them.

3 JOEY. You married her, then you did the Longshoreman's glide. Her brothers would have crippled the Daddy and Billy both if they hadn't have belonged to Joey O'Neill. I don't mind. I always knew you were a creepin' chancer, but I don't want you in my town. Anyroad, she's my girl now.

4 TERRY. What?

5 JOEY. Are your ears givin' you trouble? She's mine. So after you've served your turn tomorrow, you're out, read it? Billy, pour out a couple of large ones, son, we're going to cane them bottles. [*He looks at* TERRY.] Me and me brother are havin' a wake. Push off, no-mark!

TERRY *looks at them.* BILLY *and* JOEY *gaze back at him coldly.*

6 TERRY. And if I don't you'll 'batter me', 'cripple me', 'duff me', 'hurt me'. Well all right, I'm a physical coward. I'll do what you say.

7 JOEY. Of course you will, Hero.

8 TERRY. But get it right, you've only got your own way because it happens to be what I want. I don't need all the trappings and rituals to let me know my father's dead. You do, I don't and I'll do anything to get it over, to put as much turf between me and you lot as I can.

9 JOEY. Talk, talk.

TERRY *pauses and looks at him. When he speaks it is with quiet deliberation.*

10 TERRY. Hettie sent that boy to find you because only his sort would know where to look. I've got an address and a phone number in London and the old fella called me twice every week, Joey.

He goes out leaving them together. There is a close-up on JOEY's *face.*

22

SCENE 4   A SUITE IN THE HOTEL

Later

JUDY *is sitting in a chair. She is clad in a housecoat. There is a knock at the door. She rises and opens it, letting* TERRY *into the room.*

1   JUDY. Hello, love. You've come back early.

2   TERRY. I didn't come back. I was sent away.

3   JUDY. What?

4   TERRY. Joey sent me packing. I'm to wait his orders here. [*He flops into a deep armchair.*]

5   JUDY [*unbelieving*]. And you just left?

6   TERRY [*sadly*]. You don't understand yet, do you? If I hadn't done what he said he'd have smashed my face in with his fist. [*He has extended his own clenched fist.*] You've never seen one of these at work let alone felt it, have you? It exploded in your face like a magnesium flash, then you —then it's like a scald and it throbs with pulses of pain, you sob and it degrades you, you're like—[*He searches.*]— have you ever seen a dog run over?

7   JUDY. Stop it! It's horrible!

8   TERRY. No, it's not. It's 'proper'; it's 'tidy' and our Joey observes all the tribal customs. I'm the outsider. I'm wrong, you see. I didn't stay with my wife. It doesn't matter that I coupled with her in a back street when I was a half drunk kid. She had a baby therefore I was supposed to give her my whole life. Well, I didn't so I can be judged by Joey, all of 'em. I can do nothing right. I talk differently. I've read a book—I've no rights, no say.

9   JUDY. But couldn't you?

10 TERRY. No! 'Cos if I say one word out of place he'll hit me and I'm afraid of him—gutless afraid. So I back down. Joey's the Witch Doctor and he's rattling my father's death in my face. Well, in our tribe grievous bodily

23

harm merchants take precedence over adulterers at the
smelling out.

2 JUDY. That's a load of old rubbish and you know it.

3 TERRY. Anywhere else, any other time, yes but [*ironically*] 'the
thing which I greatly feared is come upon me, and that
which I was afraid of is come onto me'. *Job* 3:25. You see,
Joey's right by the code. He's only right.

4 JUDY. He's not and I love you.

5 TERRY. 'But that was in another country'.

6 JUDY. Then let's go back there!

7 TERRY. We will [*bleakly*]—tomorrow.

FADE OUT

Double, Double

by James Saunders

The scene is a busmen's canteen, about noon on a winter's day.

CHARACTERS

GRUNGE
NIMROD
⎫ bus drivers
GIMLET
BERT DOGG

A BUS INSPECTOR

PUMFRET, Grunge's conductor

LILLIAN, Gimlet's conductress

IRIS, Dogg's conductress

NELLIE, the cook

FRAN, the cleaner and kitchen hand

NOTE

The pairs of characters bracketed together are doubled:

GRUNGE	INSPECTOR	NIMROD
PUMFRET	BERT DOGG	GIMLET

	NELLIE	FRAN	
	LILLIAN	IRIS	

Appearance, characterization and possibly accent should be such that each member of a pair is immediately recognizable while the common identity of the pair remains obvious.

The INSPECTOR and BERT DOGG are burly men, compared with GIMLET and NIMROD. What is in IRIS a young slimness has become in FRAN an asexual wispiness. NELLIE and LILLIAN are plump.

✴ ✴ ✴
Double, Double

The main door is right and there is a window up right centre in the back wall. A door left leads to other parts of the building and a third door, behind the counter, leads to the kitchen. The counter runs parallel to the back wall from the wall left to centre, and has a flap at the right end giving access to the tables. The counter is set café-wise with biscuits, cheese rolls, etc. Behind the counter are shelves with cigarettes, matches, etc. There is a longish table right centre with two chairs above it, two chairs below it and a chair at each end. A smaller table, with four chairs, is in the corner up right. There is a hat-stand down right, a pin-table below the door left, and a clock on the wall behind the counter. Other suitable dressing may be added at the discretion of the Producer.

When the curtain rises, GRUNGE, *a bus driver, is seated alone above the right end of the table right centre, finishing his dinner, which he eats moodily, casting a dark glance now and then at the clock and then at the plate of dinner set at the place left of him. After a few moments,* NELLIE *enters behind the counter.*

1   NELLIE. What do you want for sweet?

2   GRUNGE. Is that clock right, Nellie?

3   NELLIE. It's always right. There's fruit roll or jam tart.

4   GRUNGE. Oh, I dunno. What's best?

5   NELLIE. One's hot, the other's cold.

1 GRUNGE. Hm! [*He indicates the plate of food at the place beside him.*] Here, look at this. *Look* at it.

2 NELLIE. If your mate don't get here soon, his dinner'll be cold.

3 GRUNGE. What I'm *saying*. It's congealed. Look at the time. Two jiffs, he said he'd be. 'Get my dinner for me,' he says, 'I'll be in in two jiffs.' Quarter of an hour ago, that was. I dunno what he *does* out there. [*He checks the clock against his watch.*]

4 NELLIE. Do you want it back on the hot-plate?

5 GRUNGE. Sitting there filling in his pools, I dare say.

6 NELLIE. Some people got no respect for a good meal. Might as well serve 'em bran-mash, some of 'em, they wouldn't know the difference. Look at it, going to waste. I tell you this: if he comes in complaining his dinner's cold, it'll be the finish. I've had enough complaining in this establishment. I've been back to the cardboard factory once and I can go back again, any day of the week.

7 GRUNGE. It's his stomach I'm thinking of.

8 NELLIE. Decent kitchens they got there, *and* the pay's good, *and* the hours are regular. It'll be the finish, you can tell your mate that from me.

9 GRUNGE. We're due out in a few minutes. He just plays fast and loose with his insides day after day—you'd think he'd have more sense at his age. He'll come running in here at the last minute, stuff himself full of cold potatoes and biscuits and then go straight and get it bumped about from here to Balham. No wonder he spends a fortune on Rennies.

10 NELLIE. What do you want for sweet?

11 GRUNGE. What? [*He picks up a potato from the plate beside him.*] Here, feel this. Cold as ice.

12 NELLIE. Give it here, I'll put it on the hot-plate.

GRUNGE *rises, picks up his own dirty plate and the plate of dinner and takes them to the counter.*

1   GRUNGE. What's the good of warming up the bottom of the plate? He'll regret it when he's sixty-five. Slow suicide. Give us a packet of Weights. And a box of matches.

> NELLIE *serves* GRUNGE *with the cigarettes and matches.*
> NIMROD, *a driver, enters right, overcoated and with his collar turned up. He carries a vacuum flask.*

Cold out, Nim?

2   NIMROD [*moving to the table up right*]. What the 'ell's the matter with you, then? [*He sits above the table up right.*]

3   GRUNGE. Miserable old sod! [*He pays for the cigarettes and matches.*]

4   NELLIE [*indicating the plate of food*]. What you want me to do with this, then? [*She puts the money in the till.*]

5   GRUNGE. It's as cold as it'll get. Fourteen minutes; I better go see if I can find him. Though, I don't see why I should bother. [*He crosses to the door right.*] Not my stomach he's ruining. Put it in the oven.

> NIMROD *takes a packet of sandwiches from his pocket and unwraps them.*

6   NELLIE. It'll dry up.

7   GRUNGE. Let it.

8   NELLIE. What you want for sweet?

9   GRUNGE. What's in the fruit roll?

10 NELLIE. Fruit.

11 GRUNGE. What kind of fruit?

12 NELLIE. Dried fruit.

> NIMROD *eats his sandwiches.*

13 GRUNGE. Baked, you said?

14 NELLIE. Steamed.

15 GRUNGE. Custard?

16 NELLIE. Yes.

1   GRUNGE. Jam tart.

> GRUNGE *exits right, leaving the door open.*
> NELLIE *exits to the kitchen with the dirty plate and the plate of food.*

2   NIMROD [*calling*]. What about the door, then? [*He rises and closes the door.*]

> *Before* NIMROD *has time to resume his seat, the door opens again and he pushes it.*
> FRAN *enters right carrying a bucket, mop, brush and dustpan.*

3   FRAN. Don't mind me, of course. [*She crosses to the counter, leaving the door open.*]

4   NIMROD. What about the door, then?

> FRAN *ignores* NIMROD *and puts her equipment down by the right end of the counter.* NIMROD *closes the door, resumes his seat and eats his sandwiches.*
> NELLIE *enters from the kitchen.*

5   FRAN. I saw Sid last night.

6   NELLIE. He came to see you?

7   FRAN. Oh, no, he wouldn't do that.

8   NELLIE. You didn't go round and . . .

9   FRAN. No, no. It was by accident. In a pub.

10   NELLIE. I thought you didn't go to pubs.

11   FRAN. I was with my sister.

12   NELLIE. The married one?

13   FRAN. I only got one sister. She took me out to a pub for a drink last night; to cheer me up, she said. Me and her and Don.

14   NELLIE. Who's Don?

15   FRAN. Her husband. He's on the Underground. Anyway, we was at a table in the saloon, you see, and Marge had a . . .

16   NELLIE. Who's Marge?

1   FRAN. My *sister*. Marge had a gin and tonic and Don had a brown ale and I had a gin and lime, and there we was talking about her baby . . .

2   NELLIE. Whose?

3   FRAN. *Marge's.*

4   NELLIE. I thought she didn't have one.

5   FRAN. That's the one we was talking about. And then I happened to look up and there was Sid.

6   NELLIE. Where?

7   FRAN. At the next table.

8   NELLIE. By himself?

9   FRAN. 'Don't look now, Marge,' I said, 'but look who's at the next table.' And Don said, 'Do you want to shift to the other bar?' But I said, 'No, there's no need. I'm not doing him any harm sitting here, am I?'

   A bus INSPECTOR *enters right, sits right of the table right centre and looks at the menu.*

10 NELLIE. Did he see you?

11 FRAN. Who—Sid? I dunno; he was fidgeting a bit. Anyway, after a bit I told Marge I thought I'd go over and say hallo to him. 'What', she said, 'you must be mad', she said, 'after what he's done to you.' And Don said, 'You don't want to have no more truck with him, let's move to the other bar,' he said. 'No,' I said, 'why should I? After all, I only want to say hallo to him. There's no harm in that.'

12 NELLIE. They was right; you're a fool.

13 FRAN. 'You'll make yourself cheap,' says Marge. 'You've made yourself cheap enough already,' she said. And I said, 'Well, if I have, I have; but if he owes me nothing else, at least he owes me that,' I said, 'that he'll say hallo to me at least. I can't see I'm making myself cheap saying hallo to my husband,' I said. So I got up and went over to his table and I said, 'Hallo, Sid.'

   NIMROD *rises and crosses to the door left.*

1   NIMROD. Watch my sandwiches, will you?

2   NELLIE. Why, what they going to do?

    NIMROD *exits left.*

3   FRAN. You got any tea on the go, Nellie?

    NELLIE *pours a cup of tea for* FRAN.

    'Hallo, Sid,' I said.

4   INSPECTOR [*calling*]. Sausage toad.

5   NELLIE. There ain't any.

6   INSPECTOR. It says here 'Sausage toad'.

7   NELLIE. That was yesterday.

8   INSPECTOR. What's it doing on here, then?

9   NELLIE. You want the other side.

10   INSPECTOR. Other side of what?

11   NELLIE. Turn it round.

    The INSPECTOR *turns the card.*

    Over—turn it over.

    The INSPECTOR *turns the card over.*

12   INSPECTOR. It's written upside down. [*He reverses the card.*] Ah! You want to cross it out if it's yesterday's.

13   NELLIE. It is crossed out.

14   INSPECTOR [*studying the card*]. All *right*, then. Steak and kidney pie.

15   NELLIE. None left.

16   INSPECTOR. What do you mean—'none left'?

17   NELLIE. I mean—none left. I can't help it if everyone wants steak and kidney pie.

18   INSPECTOR. You ought to foresee these things.

19   NELLIE. If you think you can do better, do the bleeding job yourself.

20   INSPECTOR. Don't you talk to me like that.

NELLIE *comes from behind the counter and crosses to the* INSPECTOR.

1 NELLIE. I've been back to the cardboard factory once, and I can go back again. Tomorrow. You keep a civil tongue in your head.

2 INSPECTOR. You'll hear about this.

3 NELLIE. What do you want to eat?

4 INSPECTOR. Haven't got much choice, have I?

5 NELLIE. No.

6 INSPECTOR. Give me the fish, then. And don't make the chips too big. I want small chips.

7 NELLIE. I'll sort 'em out for you.

NELLIE *exits behind the counter.* FRAN *picks up her tea and sits left of the table up right.*

8 INSPECTOR. The Twenty-one's twenty minutes late, the Hundred and fourteen B's thirty-five minutes late, and the Six-four-two's disappeared off the face of the earth. What do they expect of me? We've got two drivers down with jaundice, one conductor with a dislocated toe and another one having a baby. It makes you sick. [*He indicates* FRAN's *bucket.*] Someone's going to trip over that lot in a minute.

PUMFRET, *Grunge's conductor, enters right and crosses to centre.* FRAN *takes out a copy of the* Daily Mirror *and reads.*

[*to* PUMFRET] We've lost a Six-four-two.

9 PUMFRET. Where's my dinner?

10 INSPECTOR. If it doesn't turn up before you leave, you'll have to turn round at Marshall's Corner, Pumfret.

11 PUMFRET. Where's Grunge? He was supposed to save me a dinner. [*He calls.*] Nellie!

12 INSPECTOR. D'you hear what I say?

13 PUMFRET [*turning to the* INSPECTOR]. What?

14 INSPECTOR. I say since we've lost a Six-four-two . . .

15 PUMFRET. What do you mean—lost?

1 INSPECTOR. I don't know what I mean. It's gone.

2 PUMFRET. How can you lose a double-decker bus?

3 INSPECTOR. *I* haven't lost it.

4 PUMFRET. You're in charge, mate.

5 INSPECTOR. Now, look here . . .

6 PUMFRET. Where's my dinner? [*He calls.*] Nellie!

> NELLIE *enters behind the counter with a plate of fish and chips. She collects cutlery, comes from the counter and puts the food on the table in front of the* INSPECTOR.

7 NELLIE. Fish and chips.

8 PUMFRET. Where's my mate?

9 NELLIE. He's out looking for you. I don't know why you two can't never sit down together.

10 PUMFRET. I told him I'd be in.

11 INSPECTOR. Look at the size of these chips.

12 NELLIE. I picked out the smallest. They're French fried.

13 INSPECTOR. I don't care what country they are.

14 NELLIE. You provide the kitchen with a potato slicer and you'll get 'em the right size. I haven't time to go measuring them up.

15 INSPECTOR. All you've done is cut 'em in half.

16 NELLIE. French fried. [*to* PUMFRET] Yours is in the oven, drying up.

> NELLIE *exits behind the counter.*

17 PUMFRET [*sitting above the left end of the table right centre*]. Grunge is like an old woman. He'll catch his death out there looking for me, the silly old fool. He's neurotic about time; fuss, fuss, fuss.

18 INSPECTOR. I wonder she bothers to cut 'em at all.

19 PUMFRET. Here, if we're going to turn round at Marshall's Corner, what about our cup of tea.

20 INSPECTOR. What cup of tea.

1 PUMFRET. The cup of tea we shan't have at the other end.

2 INSPECTOR. You can have a cup of tea when you get back.

3 PUMFRET. Back here? You mean we're to make two journeys without a break?

4 INSPECTOR. You'll get a break.

5 PUMFRET. Where?

6 INSPECTOR. Marshall's Corner.

7 PUMFRET. There's no caff there.

8 INSPECTOR. I told you, you can have your cup of tea when you've made the round trip.

9 PUMFRET. And make two journeys one after the other without a cup of tea.

10 INSPECTOR. Look, you're only going half-way.

11 PUMFRET. Don't tell me Marshall's Corner's half-way, its more than half-way.

12 INSPECTOR. Marshall's Corner's *half-way.* Just over. Look at the times.

13 PUMFRET. Over half-way. You said it. That means there and back's more than our usual distance before we're entitled to a cup of tea. *Entitled.* Twice as much more.

14 INSPECTOR. What do you mean—'twice as much more'?

15 PUMFRET. There and back.

16 INSPECTOR [*taking out his notebook*]. Here we are. [*He refers to the book.*] Leave the garage—one-thirty-two, Marshall's Corner, two-fifty-six and you get to the other end four-fourteen.

17 PUMFRET. What does that make it?

NELLIE *enters behind the counter with a plate of steak and kidney pie and potatoes and puts it in front of* PUMFRET.

18 INSPECTOR. I'm trying to work it out.

19 PUMFRET [*looking at his meal*]. Looks a bit dry, don't it?

20 NELLIE. If you don't like it, you know what you can do. I'm not a slave to this establishment.

1 PUMFRET. Service with a smile.

   NELLIE *exits behind the counter.*

2 INSPECTOR. One hour twenty-four minutes.

3 PUMFRET. Where to?

4 INSPECTOR. Marshall's Corner.

5 PUMFRET. And what is it from there?

6 INSPECTOR. You're not going any farther.

7 PUMFRET. I just want to know.

8 INSPECTOR. One hour eighteen.

9 PUMFRET. There you are.

10 INSPECTOR. What.

11 PUMFRET. Six minutes difference.

12 INSPECTOR. Six minutes won't kill you, will it?

13 PUMFRET. Six minutes is all right. But this is twelve.There and back. The journey's too long as it is, you know that as well as I do.

14 INSPECTOR. But you'll have a *break* half-way.

15 PUMFRET. More than half-way.

16 INSPECTOR. Half-way.

17 PUMFRET. There's six minutes . . .

18 INSPECTOR. Half-way there and back.

19 PUMFRET. Without a cup of tea. And what happens if I want to go to the lav? There's nothing at Marshall's Corner.

20 INSPECTOR. There never has been.

21 PUMFRET. Well then!

22 INSPECTOR. Well, then, you can do what you usually do.

23 PUMFRET. I usually wait till the other end.

24 INSPECTOR. Then you can wait till you get back here, can't you? And have it with your tea.

25 PUMFRET. You expect me to hang on for an extra twelve minutes?

1 INSPECTOR. Six minutes.

2 PUMFRET. Twelve! There and back.

3 INSPECTOR. But you don't want to go till you get there.

4 PUMFRET. How do you know when I'll want to go? [*He pauses.*]
    This is sheer regimentation.

5 INSPECTOR. You know what you're being, you're being
    obstructionist.

6 PUMFRET. Oh, really!

7 INSPECTOR. I've had buses turn round at Marshall's Corner
    time after time before now. And nothing said.

8 PUMFRET. Ah, but you forget one thing. Times have changed.
    Bus crews are in short supply. The old days are gone,
    mate. We don't strain our bladders for anyone.

    There is a pause.

9 INSPECTOR. All right, then. All right, then. We know where
    we stand.

10 PUMFRET. That's right.

    There is a pause. They eat.

    Mind *you*, if you want a help out, I don't mind turning
    round at Marshall's Corner.

    The INSPECTOR *lowers his fork.*

    After all, we're all in it together, aren't we, mate?
    'Course, I can't speak for my driver; Grunge isn't easy
    like me. I suppose I'd better hurry up and find him.
    Tell him to stop looking for me. [*He takes a potato.*]

11 INSPECTOR. Here!

12 PUMFRET. What's up?

13 INSPECTOR. What's that on your plate?

14 PUMFRET. I dunno. Looks like steak and kidney pie. I only eat
    the potatoes.

    The INSPECTOR *rises and goes to the counter.*

37

1 INSPECTOR [*calling*]. Nellie.

> NELLIE *enters behind the counter.*

2 NELLIE. What?

3 INSPECTOR. I thought you said the pie was finished. [*He points to* PUMFRET's *plate.*] What's that over there, then?

4 NELLIE. That's the last of it.

5 INSPECTOR. But he came in after me.

6 NELLIE. It was ordered.

7 INSPECTOR. He's not even eating it.

8 NELLIE. Then what are you complaining about? Anything else?

9 INSPECTOR. Give us a cup of tea.

> NELLIE *pours a cup of tea for the* INSPECTOR.

> [*He casts around and sees* FRAN.] Are you supposed to be sweeping up, or aren't you?

> FRAN *finishes her tea, rises, collects her broom and begins to sweep.* PUMFRET *rises, picks up his plate, moves and puts it on the counter.*

10 PUMFRET. Can't eat any more of that. Give us a couple of packets of biscuits, Nell. And some Rennies.

11 NELLIE. Setlers.

12 PUMFRET. They'll do. All grist to the mill. [*He puts a ten-shilling note on the counter.*] Take it out of that.

> NELLIE *quickly serves* PUMFRET *with his biscuits and Setlers, puts the note in the till and gives him his change, then exits behind the counter.*

13 INSPECTOR. Why have it if you don't want it? There's other people . . .

> FRAN *stops sweeping and watches.*

14 PUMFRET. I like the gravy. If Grunge comes in, I'm looking for him. [*He crosses to the door.*]

1 INSPECTOR. Sheer criminal waste. Don't forget about Marshall's Corner, then.

PUMFRET stops, turns and moves to the INSPECTOR.

2 PUMFRET. Time was when bus crews did what they was told and no questions asked. We was ten a penny, see? But times have changed; we're on top now.

3 INSPECTOR. Well?

4 PUMFRET. That's why we can afford to be magnanimous—as long as no one thinks it's creating a precedent. Don't *you* forget *that*.

PUMFRET exits right, singing.

5 INSPECTOR [*rounding on* FRAN]. What do you think you're gawping at? [*He picks up his tea and resumes his seat at the table right centre.*]

FRAN crosses and sweeps down left.
GIMLET, a driver, and LILLIAN, *his conductress, enter right.* LILLIAN *carries her handbag and a book.* GIMLET *removes his coat and cap.* LILLIAN *crosses and is about to put her bag and book on the chair below the left end of the table right centre, but* GIMLET *forestalls her and flings his coat and cap on the chair.* LILLIAN *moves and puts her book and bag on the chair left of the table up right.*

[*He looks at his watch. To* GIMLET] Well, at least *you're* on time.

6 GIMLET. I'm always on time. What are you getting at?

7 INSPECTOR. All I said . . .

8 GIMLET. Have you ever known me not on time? You want to make a complaint?

9 INSPECTOR. Now, look here . . .

10 GIMLET. Though I tell you this: if I *was* late in today, I'd have every excuse. I've had nothing but obstruction, obstruction, from first to last.

11 LILLIAN [*moving above the table right centre*]. If you mean by obstruction a few old ladies waiting at request stops, that you couldn't bother to pull up for . . .

1 GIMLET [*sitting left of the table right centre*]. She wasn't waiting at a request stop, she was on the other side of the road.

2 LILLIAN. She was half-way across and waving her umbrella. It was quite obvious she wanted to get on.

FRAN stops sweeping and listens.

3 GIMLET. Oh, get lost!

4 LILLIAN. Poor old lady; to leave her standing there in the cold . . .

5 GIMLET. She wasn't old! She was middle-bloody-aged!

6 LILLIAN. How do you know? We went past at forty miles an hour.

7 GIMLET. Am I to stop every time some old dear waves an umbrella in the distance?

8 LILLIAN. I think it's disgusting. We are the servants of the public.

9 GIMLET. Wrap up, will you? Let's have a rest from each other for half an hour.

10 LILLIAN [*moving to the door right*]. As for *why* you're so keen to be back on time—we all know the reason for that.

LILLIAN exits right.

11 GIMLET. Why don't you drop dead!

But the door has closed behind her.

12 INSPECTOR. What's this, then?

13 GIMLET [*calling*]. Nellie! [*to FRAN*] Where is that woman?

14 FRAN. She's gone.

15 GIMLET. I want something to eat.

16 FRAN. She's having her lunch.

17 GIMLET. And what am I supposed to do?

FRAN puts down her broom and goes behind the counter.

18 FRAN. Fish and chips or pie?

19 NELLIE [*off; calling*]. There's no pie.

1 FRAN. There's no pie. Fish and chips or nothing.

2 GIMLET. All right, then.

3 FRAN. All right—what?

4 GIMLET. All right—fish and chips.

FRAN *exits behind the counter.*

5 INSPECTOR. They're not chips, neither. They're boiled potatoes cut in half and dropped into lukewarm fat.

6 GIMLET. I don't care what I eat. Got no appetite, anyway.

7 INSPECTOR. What's all this about request stops, then? And
forty mile an hour?

8 GIMLET. I want to change my conductor. I've had enough, do
you hear? I don't care who I go out with, but I'm not
going out again with that woman. I don't know what it
is but every time she rings the bell I feel like running the
bus through a shop window. We're incompatible.

9 INSPECTOR. Have you been ignoring request stops, or haven't
you?

10 GIMLET. If anyone wants to lay a complaint let 'em lay a
complaint.

11 INSPECTOR. Speeding's a serious offence.

12 GIMLET. I wish someone would. You hear that? I wish
someone would get me the sack so I could scrape the
dust of this concern off my feet and get back to making
doughnuts again.

13 INSPECTOR. Nobody's keeping you here against your will. If
you don't like the job . . .

14 GIMLET. All right, all right. [*He pauses.*] I didn't see the Six-
four-two when I came in.

15 INSPECTOR. No.

16 GIMLET. Should have been in twenty minutes ago.

17 INSPECTOR. That's right.

18 GIMLET. Can't have gone out again.

19 INSPECTOR. No.

1 GIMLET. Well?

2 INSPECTOR. Hasn't been in.

3 GIMLET. Twenty minutes late?

4 INSPECTOR. Twenty-two and a half.

5 GIMLET. How's that, then?

6 INSPECTOR. That's right.

7 GIMLET. I said, 'How's that, then'?

8 INSPECTOR. I dunno. [*He eats stolidly.*]

9 GIMLET. Don't give me a clue, will you?

10 INSPECTOR. Why do you want to know. Want to take my job over?

11 GIMLET. But it's the quietest service in the district.

12 INSPECTOR. That's right.

13 GIMLET. And a straight road all the way from Marshall's Corner.

14 INSPECTOR. That's right.

15 GIMLET. So he's broken it down, has he?

16 INSPECTOR. Who?

17 GIMLET. Dogg. Bert Dogg, the bloke who calls himself the driver. He's done it on purpose.

18 INSPECTOR. Who done what?

19 GIMLET. What did he give it—a puncture?

20 INSPECTOR. Pass the vinegar.

21 GIMLET. Was it?

22 INSPECTOR. Pass the vinegar.

GIMLET *passes the vinegar.*

'Tasn't broken down.

23 GIMLET. What then?

24 INSPECTOR. It's gone.

25 GIMLET. What do you mean—gone?

26 INSPECTOR. Gone.

1 GIMLET. For the love of Mike . . .

2 INSPECTOR. Disappeared. It's not on the rout.

3 GIMLET. You've lost a double-decker bus!

4 INSPECTOR. Now look here, I've had enough of this. You all think I've got a cushy number, don't you? I know what's said about me behind my back. Well, just you try my job for a change, that's all. Go on, try it. Here, take me cap. And here's me book. You go and see if you can do better. I tell you, there's nothing but grouse, grouse on this job from the lot of you, crews, passengers, the lot— grouse, grouse, grouse. You grouse if I change the time-tables and if I leave things as they are you still grouse. I'm sick of the lot of you; you're nothing but a lot of—of —of left-wingers.

5 GIMLET. Don't you call me a left-winger.

6 INSPECTOR. What else are you, then, eh, what else?

7 GIMLET. My union'll hear about this.

8 INSPECTOR. Take my book, go on, take it.

9 GIMLET. I don't want your blasted book!

> *There is a pause. The* INSPECTOR *and* GIMLET *look murderously at each other, then both rise and move silently to the counter.*
> FRAN *enters behind the counter.*

[*to* FRAN] Where's my bleeding dinner?

10 FRAN. There wasn't no more chips. Nellie just had the last of 'em.

11 GIMLET. So what am I supposed to do?

12 FRAN. Wait ten minutes.

> GIMLET *crosses and wanders out right.*

13 INSPECTOR. Tomato sauce.

14 FRAN. O.K. [*She passes him a bottle of O.K. sauce from the shelves behind her.*]

15 INSPECTOR. I said 'tomato'.

16 FRAN. O.K. We've only got O.K., I'm telling you.

1 INSPECTOR. All right.

2 FRAN. O.K.

> FRAN *exits behind the counter.*
> GRUNGE *enters right and crosses to centre.*

3 GRUNGE. I can't find my conductor.

4 INSPECTOR. He's out looking for you.

5 GRUNGE. It's like a bloody merry-go-round. [*He crosses to the door right.*]

6 INSPECTOR. I want you to turn round at Marshall's Corner this trip, Grunge.

> GRUNGE *stops and turns.*

7 GRUNGE. What about our cup of tea?

8 INSPECTOR. See Pumfret about it.

> GRUNGE *exits right. The* INSPECTOR *resumes his seat right of the table right centre and pours sauce on his meal as though emptying it down a sink.*
> GIMLET *enters right.*

9 GIMLET [*crossing and sitting left of the table right centre*]. No sign of it.

10 INSPECTOR. What?

11 GIMLET. The bus.

12 INSPECTOR. 'Tain't your worry. [*He pauses.*] It wasn't always like this.

13 GIMLET. Like what?

14 INSPECTOR. Like it is now.

15 GIMLET. I wouldn't know.

16 INSPECTOR. Well, I'm telling you. It wasn't always like this. Once they was dedicated men.

17 GIMLET. Go on!

18 INSPECTOR. In nineteen-thirty-eight there was a driver, name of Hackett, was climbing into his cab at the change-over at Parson's Green when he slipped and fractured the big toe on his left foot. What d'you think he did?

1 GIMLET. Fractured the big toe of his . . .

2 INSPECTOR. All right, listen: he drove that bus all the way
back to the depot, though every change of gear was
sheer agony. Turned up dead on schedule. 'The bus had
to get through', he said. Dedication.

3 GIMLET. What did he get out of it?

4 INSPECTOR. He was highly commended.

5 GIMLET. How much is that in pounds?

6 INSPECTOR. Strike a light! You blokes today . . .

7 GIMLET. I'm not going to argue the toss about it. [*He pauses.*]
So he's taken the bus, has he? That's going a bit far.

8 INSPECTOR. Who?

9 GIMLET. Bert Dogg, of course. Taken her off in a double-
decker bus.

10 INSPECTOR. What's it to do with you, anyway?

11 GIMLET. As a matter of fact, I had something to say to a
member of the crew.

12 INSPECTOR. Not Dogg, I take it.

13 GIMLET. I've nothing to say to Dogg. Him and me don't
speak the same language.

14 INSPECTOR. Ho, ho, I see.

15 GIMLET. I've only got half an hour; he knows that, of course.
He's checked up. Or they've put him on to it.

16 INSPECTOR. Who's 'they'?

17 GIMLET. Them. You realize, I suppose, that this is no accident.
He was destined to run off with that bus; it was in the
stars.

18 INSPECTOR. Are you mad?

19 GIMLET. Maybe I am at that. I tell you this: I'm sick of this job.
I've had enough of it, the lot. End of the week I get me
cards. I don't give a bugger if the bus comes in or not.
[*He rises.*] Think I'll go down to the office and see if
there's any word. [*He crosses to the door right.*]

20 INSPECTOR. That's what I like to see. Dedication.

GIMLET exits right, slamming the door behind him. There is a pause. FRAN enters behind the counter and stands above the table right centre.

1 FRAN. I saw Sid last night.

2 INSPECTOR. What?

3 FRAN. I saw Sid last night.

4 INSPECTOR. What's for sweet?

5 FRAN [*indicating the menu*]. It's writ on there.

The INSPECTOR picks up the menu and looks at it.

6 INSPECTOR. Syrup pudding. Only I don't want any syrup with it. You get me? I just want the pudding. Middle cut. I don't want an end piece. [*sarcastically*] You think you can do that?

7 FRAN. No.

8 INSPECTOR. Why not?

9 FRAN. You got the wrong side of the menu again.

There is a pause. The INSPECTOR turns the menu over.

10 INSPECTOR. Fruit roll, then.

11 FRAN. Off.

12 INSPECTOR. Now, look here . . .

13 FRAN. Nellie's just had the last piece. I can't call it back, can I?

14 INSPECTOR. Bring me the jam tart.

FRAN picks up the INSPECTOR's empty plate and moves behind the counter.

Without custard.

15 FRAN. I'm not sure we got any without custard. We got some custard without tart.

FRAN exits behind the counter.
NIMROD enters right, sits at his table up right and eats his sandwiches.

16 NIMROD. Cold out there. We're in for some slush soon.

46

1 INSPECTOR [*rising, moving to left of the table up right and facing* NIMROD]. You mean snow?

2 NIMROD. It turns to slush, don't it? Let's not kid ourselves. All this Christmas card stuff. If I had my way, you know what Christmas cards would have on them? Slush.

LILLIAN enters right, closes the door and crosses to the counter.

[*without looking up from his sandwiches*] What about the door, then?

3 LILLIAN. It happens to be closed.

4 NIMROD [*to the* INSPECTOR]. Sky's like porridge. Sleet sky, that's what that is. And tonight it'll freeze. Be murder on the roads in the morning. And that east wind goes right through you.

5 INSPECTOR. Last summer you was complaining about the heat.

6 NIMROD. We didn't have any summer.

7 INSPECTOR. You was complaining about it, all the same. Trouble with you, you don't eat proper food. What good are sandwiches? You want a hot meal.

8 NIMROD. I get a hot meal at home.

9 INSPECTOR. Want to get something hot down you, midday. Have some fish and chips.

10 NIMROD. Don't like fish and chips. I only like sausage and mash.

11 INSPECTOR. How can you only like sausage and mash?

12 NIMROD. No law against it, is there?

13 INSPECTOR. You mean to say you never eat nothing else?

14 NIMROD. Why should I? I don't like anything else.

15 INSPECTOR. Every day you have . . .?

16 NIMROD. Do you mind!

17 INSPECTOR. What does your wife think about that?

18 NIMROD. What she thinks is her business. She used to try it on, once upon a time. Used to cook fancy stuff, veal

cutlets and muck, but I soon put a stop to that. 'You can put this back where it came from,' I said to her, 'you know what I like and that's what I'm going to get, from now on, and none of your half-larks,' I said. 'What', she said, 'every day?' 'Yes,' I said, 'why not? If I like it why shouldn't I have it every day?' 'You'll get sick of it,' she said. 'Now, look here,' I said, 'when I get sick of it I'll say so. Until then,' I said, 'I'm going to have it. Every day.' 'And what about me?' she said.'What do you mean, "what about you?"' I said. 'I mean, am I to have no say in it?' she said. 'Say?' I said. 'Yes,' she said, 'do you expect me to have it every day whether I want it or not?' 'What's the matter,' I said, 'don't you like it?' 'Not every day,' she said. 'Well, listen here,' I said, 'you better get this straight. I want it every day and I'm going to have it every day, and if I don't get it from you I'll get it from someone else.' 'What do you mean by that?' she said. 'Fred's caff,' I said, 'that's what I mean. I can get it from Fred's caff any day of the week. I know the girl behind the counter.'

2   INSPECTOR. What about Christmas?

3   NIMROD. What about it? Not my fault, is it?

4   INSPECTOR. You have sausage and mash at Christmas?

5   NIMROD. Why not? Stick a bit of holly in it.

6   LILLIAN [calling]. Am I to have any service?

    FRAN enters behind the counter.

7   FRAN. Fish and chips.

8   LILLIAN. Or what?

9   FRAN. Or nothing.

10   LILLIAN. What sort of fish is it?

11   FRAN. Fried fish.

12   LILLIAN. Fried what?

13   FRAN. Fish.

14   LILLIAN. But what? Plaice, cod, haddock?

1   FRAN. You mean—before it was fried?

2   LILLIAN. It doesn't matter.

3   FRAN. Nellie might have known. [*She calls.*] Nellie!

There is no answer.

No answer.

4   LILLIAN. It doesn't *matter*.

5   FRAN. Fish and chips, then. It'll be five minutes.

FRAN *exits behind the counter.*

6   LILLIAN. I wonder why everything has to be so—shabby. Dismal. Temporary. I'm sure it's quite unnecessary. This should be an age of consummation, full of light and grace. Here we are, past the middle of the twentieth century. With all that implies. The prospects are un- limited. And what comes out of it. Fish and chips or nothing. Sauce bottles congealed at the top. Zinc alloy forks with twisted prongs. Rubber bread. Plastic table- cloths. Who could have imagined it, fifty years ago? 'What?' I can hear them saying, 'With atomic energy and humanism? All will be light and air and cultured ease.' Not that I'm complaining. On the contrary; complaining, or rather the attitude of mind that goes with it, is the cause of all the trouble. If people com- plained less they'd have more time to open their eyes to what we have and what we need; what we have and should be thankful for, and what we need and should work for. We need a positive attitude, we need joy. Though where it's to come from it's hard to say.

7   NIMROD. You talking to me?

8   LILLIAN. To no one in particular.

9   NIMROD. You want to wait till you get to my age, my girl. Then you'll see.

10 LILLIAN. See what? What'll I see?

11 NIMROD. Nothing.

12 INSPECTOR. Atomic energy's one thing, bus time-tables are another. [*He turns to the counter and calls.*] Fran!

49

FRAN *enters behind the counter.*

Where's my jam tart, then?

2   FRAN. Ooh, I forgot.

FRAN *exits behind the counter. The* INSPECTOR *resumes his seat right of the table right centre.*

3   LILLIAN. On the contrary . . .

4   INSPECTOR. What?

5   LILLIAN [*moving to left of the table right centre*]. On the contrary, they're both part of the twentieth century. Why should one be up-to-date and the other archaic?

6   INSPECTOR. Now, look here . . .

7   LILLIAN. It's absolutely ridiculous. Little men in long over-coats standing on street corners with their little time-tables—stagecoach technique pure and simple. And what happens? You lose buses.

8   INSPECTOR. Now, look here . . .

9   LILLIAN. You see, all you can ever say is 'look here'. You've no defence for the system.

10 INSPECTOR. I suppose you think it's a cushy job standing on street corners?

11 LILLIAN. You miss the point.

12 INSPECTOR. You want to try it, that's all, just try it. Go out there in the drizzle and try it.

13 LILLIAN. That isn't the *point*.

14 INSPECTOR. Ah! No! You'd say 'point' if you was out there with frozen fingers. You'd talk about 'point'.

15 LILLIAN. Oh, dear, oh, dear.

16 INSPECTOR. You'd say 'oh, dear, oh, dear,' if you was out there.

17 LILLIAN. 'Nothing but misery all around I see . . .'

18 INSPECTOR. You'd see it if you was out there. Where's my sweet, then?

FRAN *enters behind the counter with a plate of jam tart and custard and collects a spoon and fork.*

1 NIMROD. There's no joy in any of it.

2 LILLIAN. That depends on the person, if I may say so.

3 NIMROD. All right, just wait. Twenty years, that's all, just twenty years.

FRAN puts the sweet in front of the INSPECTOR.

4 LILLIAN. Wait for what?

5 NIMROD. You'll see.

6 INSPECTOR. What's this, then? I said 'no custard'.

7 FRAN. I couldn't take it off once it's on, could I? It's all soaked in.

FRAN moves behind the counter. NIMROD screws up the top on his vacuum flask, folds up and pockets his wrappers, and rises.

8 NIMROD [*moving to the counter*]. Light and *what?* [*to* FRAN] Ten Woods. [*to* LILLIAN] Grace? Light and grace?

FRAN serves NIMROD with the cigarettes. He puts down the money and waits for the change. FRAN puts the money in the till and the change on the counter.

[*to* LILLIAN] Not married, are you?

9 LILLIAN. That has nothing to do with it. [*She moves and sits left of the table up right.*]

10 NIMROD. Ha, ha! [*He picks up his change, moves to* LILLIAN, *fishes his wallet out of an inside pocket, opens it, pulls out a photograph and shows it to her.*] Look at that.

11 LILLIAN. What is it?

12 NIMROD. Me. Nineteen-thirty-five. Taken on Beachy Head. Member of the Socialist Party, I was. Didn't believe in money. Everything was going to be fine. I was just waiting for the day. [*He replaces the photograph and wallet in his pocket.*]

13 LILLIAN. You've missed the point.

NIMROD crosses to the door right then stops and turns.

14 NIMROD. What point? What the hell point?

NIMROD *exits right.* LILLIAN *opens her book.*

1 INSPECTOR. He don't eat properly. That's his trouble.

FRAN *enters behind the counter with a plate of fish and chips. She collects cutlery and puts the meal on the table in front of* LILLIAN.

2 FRAN. Fish and chips.

3 LILLIAN. Thank you.

FRAN *sits above the table up right.*

4 FRAN. Did I ever tell you about Sid?

5 LILLIAN. Yes.

6 FRAN. Well, I saw him last night.

7 LILLIAN. Really?

8 FRAN. In a pub. I was with my sister Marge and her husband. And I happened to look up and there he was.

9 LILLIAN [*after a pause*]. Who?

10 FRAN. Sid. Only he didn't see me, or anyway he kept his eyes away. He was with someone else, you see. No one I knew. She may not even have known about me. I mean, he could have kept quiet about it. After all, he might not want to have to go explaining how things are every time he meets someone. Not at first, anyway. Just as well to keep it dark, perhaps.

11 LILLIAN. You're too easy.

12 FRAN. That's what Marge says, but I don't see it. Anyway, I thought I'd go over and say hallo to him.

13 LILLIAN. After what he's done to you?

14 FRAN. He didn't do nothing to me. Only left me. It's a free country. [*She pauses.*] After all, he must have wanted to.

15 LILLIAN. What?

16 FRAN. Leave me. To *leave* me. You can't help what you want, can you? I wouldn't like to think of his staying on with me if he didn't want to.

17 LILLIAN. Why not, if it's his duty?

1 FRAN. I don't know nothing about duty. So, as I say, I thought I'd go up and say hallo to him.

2 LILLIAN [*after a pause*]. Well?

3 FRAN. So I did.

4 INSPECTOR. Cup of tea.

5 FRAN [*rising*]. I went across to where he was sitting with this friend, and I stood there and he still didn't see me, or at least he didn't seem to, and I said: 'Hallo, Sid,' I said.

6 INSPECTOR. With sugar.

> FRAN *collects the* INSPECTOR'S *empty plate, goes behind the counter and pours a cup of tea.*
> PUMFRET *enters right.*

7 PUMFRET [*crossing to centre*]. Well, here we are again.

8 INSPECTOR. Pumfret! What the devil are you doing here? Why aren't you on the rout?

9 PUMFRET. It was coming on to rain, so we decided not to go.

10 INSPECTOR. Have you gone mad?

11 PUMFRET. Keep your hair on; it was an act of God.

12 INSPECTOR. What are you talking about.

13 PUMFRET. He gave us a flat tyre.

14 INSPECTOR. Good Lord!

15 PUMFRET. I left Grunge at the helm while they change the wheel. Grunge never deserts a sinking ship. Cup of tea, please, Fran.

16 INSPECTOR. It all just transpires against me, that's what it does. Transpires. [*He rises and moves to the door right.*]

17 FRAN. What about your tea?

18 PUMFRET. It's all right. I'll drink it.

> GIMLET *enters right.*

19 GIMLET. There's no word of that bus.

20 INSPECTOR. What do you expect me to do about it?

The INSPECTOR *exits right.*
FRAN *exits behind the counter.* PUMFRET *picks up the cup of tea and sits above the left end of the table right centre.*

1 GIMLET. 'Course it's nothing to do with you if a bus vanishes into thin air. How I hate that bloke.

2 LILLIAN. Is there anyone you don't hate?

GIMLET *glares balefully at* LILLIAN *and crosses to the counter.*

Bus inspectors; old ladies at request stops . . .

3 GIMLET. If you think I'm spending my dinner break arguing the toss with you, you're wrong.

4 LILLIAN. You hate everybody. Even yourself, I dare say. Not that I'd blame you for that.

5 GIMLET. Put another record on. [*He paces up and down left.*]

FRAN *enters behind the counter with a plate of fish and chips, which she puts on the counter.*

[*He looks at his watch.*] My last chance for a fortnight. Oh, he's clever is Dogg. I could wring his neck. The feeling of having his throat between my fingers . . .

6 FRAN. Don't you want your dinner?

7 GIMLET. What?

8 FRAN. Your fish.

9 GIMLET [*moving to the counter*]. All right, give it here. Suppose I'd better eat it. [*He collects the food and some cutlery and sits morosely left of the table right centre, but does not eat.*]

10 PUMFRET. Life goes on, mate.

11 GIMLET. Hm!

12 PUMFRET. Sometimes it gets worse and sometimes it don't.

13 GIMLET. When I want philosophy I'll ask you for it.

14 PUMFRET. That's not philosophy, it's fact. The fruit of my experience. When you get to my age . . .

15 GIMLET. With any luck I shan't, shall I? [*He pauses.*] You want my dinner?

1 PUMFRET. Don't you want it?

2 GIMLET. I wouldn't give it away if I did, would I?

3 PUMFRET. You worried about the H-bomb?

4 GIMLET. Bugger the H-bomb!

5 PUMFRET. I thought you weren't. Love, eh?

6 GIMLET. What are you talking about?

7 PUMFRET. I'll just have some of the batter. [*He helps himself.*]

8 GIMLET [*looking at his watch*]. Nineteen minutes left.

9 PUMFRET. I was that way once. She worked in a tobacconist's. Her name was Peggy. It was terrible; I couldn't sleep, had no appetite. It's a funny business. Unreasonable you know. Look at this. [*He takes out a photograph and shows it to* GIMLET.] Well?

10 GIMLET. Well—what?

11 PUMFRET. That was Peggy.

12 GIMLET. What am I supposed to do?

13 PUMFRET. What do you think of her?

14 GIMLET. Nothing.

15 PUMFRET. You've hit the nail on the head. That's just the way I feel. I look at this photo and I think, 'Well, there's a fine example of nothing at all.'

16 LILLIAN [*to* FRAN]. May I have a cup of coffee, please?

FRAN *pours a cup of coffee for* LILLIAN.

17 PUMFRET. Mind *you, that* was nearly ten years ago. She had me, then. For six months she had me. I was so taken up with her I even introduced her to my wife. [*He takes out another photograph.*] There they both are—side by side. That's our back garden. We had a nice show of wallflowers that year. We used to play rummy together, the three of us. And then one day I suddenly realized I was getting more of a kick out of the rummy than I was from Peggy. So that was that.

FRAN *takes the coffee to* LILLIAN *then returns behind the counter.*

1   GIMLET. Then why carry her photo about?

2   PUMFRET. To remind me. Whenever I see something that takes my fancy, I take this out and look at it and I say to myself, 'Don't kid yourself, mate. Give her six months and this'll be her—a wonderful example of absolutely nothing.' [*He pockets the photographs and helps himself to more batter.*] Looks sort of naked with its batter off, don't it?

   GIMLET *rises and goes to the counter.*

3   GIMLET [*to* FRAN]. Give us a cup of tea.

4   FRAN. I saw Sid last night.

5   GIMLET. Oh, for the love of Mike! [*He moves down left.*]

   FRAN *pours a cup of tea.*

6   LILLIAN. Boor. Boor.

7   GIMLET [*turning to* LILLIAN]. Look, in something over quarter of an hour we've got to share the same bus. Meanwhile, perhaps you could keep out of my hair. I'm sick, sick, sick of this. [*He goes to the pin-table and puts a penny in.*]

8   FRAN. D'you want your tea?

9   GIMLET. No.

10 LILLIAN [*quietly*]. Boor. Boor.

   GIMLET *slams the pin-table. The 'tilt' sign lights up.*

11 GIMLET. Sod all pin-tables! [*He turns away and resumes his seat left of the table right centre. To* PUMFRET] You've got it all wrong, mate.

12 PUMFRET. What?

13 GIMLET. About this girl.

14 PUMFRET [*rising*]. I'll have that tea if you don't want it. [*He collects the cup of tea from the counter and resumes his seat.*]

15 GIMLET. I can get women any day of the week. Look, I've got three on the go at *present.*

   PUMFRET *drinks his tea.*

You ever worked in a bakery?

2 PUMFRET. No.

3 GIMLET. I was apprenticed. My old man's idea. 'Whatever happens,' he said, 'there'll always be bread. You work hard,' he used to say, 'keep your nose clean, don't sauce your superiors, do as you're told and never do nothing anyone can take exception to. And if it's ever a choice between shining like a star and being ordinary, you be dead ordinary,' he said. 'And in ten years you'll have a nice steady job with a nice steady wage and no one can touch you.' Six years I had of long tins and small tins and coburgs and Vienna rotten twists. I stuck it. Then they put me on doughnuts. All night long I used to turn out doughnuts. I stank of doughnuts. I had three weeks of it and then I went to the boss. 'What's the matter?' he says, 'Don't you like making doughnuts?' 'How can you *like* making doughnuts?' I said, 'How can anyone like making doughnuts? What do you take me for,' I said, 'a cretin? You think I'm like the rest of them in there?' I said, 'Because I'll tell you what they are, they're a bunch of bloody nitwits. Just tell me this,' I said, 'perhaps I'm missing something, maybe I'm stupid; but what am I supposed to be getting out of making doughnuts for you?' 'There's plenty to take the job over if you don't want it,' he said. 'Is there? Right. Fine. In that case', I said, 'you can do you-know-what with your bakehouse and your doughnuts, as well, one by one, because I'm getting out from under.' I lost my temper, see? I'd had enough.

LILLIAN *finishes her meal, rises, goes to the counter and pays* FRAN.

4 LILLIAN. I'm going for a walk.

5 GIMLET. What am I supposed to do? Chase you?

6 LILLIAN. It's immaterial to me.

LILLIAN *exits right.*

7 FRAN [*putting the money in the till*]. In that case, I suppose I can have my dinner. Nellie'll be finished.

FRAN *exits behind the counter.*

1 GIMLET. Do you ever have a feeling you're being got at?

2 PUMFRET. Who by?

3 GIMLET. How do I know? *Them.* Things keep getting in your hair. Whatever you try to do goes sour on you.

4 PUMFRET. Why you, specially?

5 GIMLET. I don't know. There's blokes worked in that bakehouse year in year out, living so ordinary you could scream. Yet they never feel they've been got at. Well, then, if I'm not being got at who's getting at me to make me feel I *am* being got at? I tell you, sometimes I just want to find something to take a sock at.

6 PUMFRET. It's love, mate. It mixes things up.

7 GIMLET. I tell you it's not love. You've got it all wrong. Look, I took Iris out a couple of times not long after I started at this job. The pictures and that. She's a nice kid in her way, and I don't like going to the pictures on my own, especially when they're crummy as they usually are. All right, and then the next time I want to take her to some crummy film she's had her schedule changed, so I can't. So be it, it's no skin off my nose, except I don't like having my plans mucked up, see? So I try to arrange some other time. And I find whenever I'm working early she's working late, and when she's working early *I'm* working late. This irritates me, you see; it don't matter, but it *irritates* me. Well, we finally coincide again, and on the night I'm to go out with her her mother gets taken bad at Woking and she takes a fortnight off to look after her. You can't blame her for that, can you? I hang on till she comes back, and then I try to bump into her at the depot so I can arrange to take her to the pictures. Only we never quite seem to get to the depot at the same time. And when I finally do see her, she's working late again and I'm working early. Meanwhile, I find she's being taken out by this bloke Dogg, and if there's anyone I can't stand it's this bloke *Dogg.*

8 PUMFRET. Why?

1   GIMLET. I don't know. I've nothing against him. I just hate his guts. No reason why he shouldn't take her out, it makes no odds to me. It's just a bit galling not to be able to do a simple thing like take a girl you don't even much care about to the *pictures*. So I find I'm spending all my time looking up bus times and cinema times like Napoleon planning a battle and I'm even less satisfied with my lot than I was at the doughnuts. So I tell myself I'll have one last go and if I find I'm still being got at I'll cut my losses and go back to baking. On consulting my charts I find we're both due in together today, that is now, we're both off early tomorrow night, and the local cinema hasn't up to the present moment either blown up or burnt down. So I make it my business to get in on schedule, in spite of sundry old dears with tortoise disease who've been planted at request stops all along the route so as to flag me down with their umbrellas and then change their minds when I've stopped. And in spite of a certain female conductress who likes to give the passengers time to settle down and take off their shoes and admire the scenery before she deigns to ring the bell. And when I get here against all the odds, what do I find? Only that that—bastard Dogg —has taken his bus together with Iris and gone off on holiday with it. I'd fixed everything else, you see. But I hadn't thought of him taking the bus and all.

There is a pause. PUMFRET *rises, moves left centre and stands looking at* GIMLET *for a few moments.*

2   PUMFRET. You was born under the wrong star, mate.

PUMFRET crosses and exits right.
NELLIE enters behind the counter and busies herself collecting the dirty plates, etc., and putting them on the counter.

3   NELLIE [*collecting* GIMLET's *plate*]. You made a right mess of this fish, haven't you? Waste of good protein, that is.

4   GIMLET. It hasn't been touched. Put more batter round it.

The INSPECTOR *enters right.*

1 INSPECTOR [*moving above the table right centre*]. I've found where it is.

2 GIMLET. You don't say!

3 INSPECTOR. Don't you want to know?

4 GIMLET. What the hell's it to me?

The INSPECTOR *turns away.*

All right, where is it, then?

GRUNGE *enters right.*

5 GRUNGE. I've lost my mate again.

6 INSPECTOR. Haven't you gone, yet?

7 GRUNGE. I've been sitting there freezing. We've had the wheel on five minutes ago. Can't go with no conductor, can I?

8 INSPECTOR. Look in the lav.

9 GRUNGE. You'd think he was avoiding me.

GRUNGE *exits right.*

10 INSPECTOR. All the spirit's gone out of public transport. No *esprit de corpse* nowadays. Might as well all wrap up and go home.

11 GIMLET. Where is it?

12 INSPECTOR. You know Dogg used to be on the number Fourteens? Single-decker rout—turns off right at Marshall's Corner.

PUMFRET *enters right.*

13 PUMFRET. That wheel done, yet?

14 INSPECTOR. It's been on five minutes. Your driver's looking for you.

15 PUMFRET. I'm off, then. If he comes in again—I've gone.

PUMFRET *exits right.*

16 INSPECTOR. It has to be a single-decker rout, you see, for the simple reason is, there's a low bridge across the road.

Barely fourteen foot headroom. Well, it seems Dogg had a lapse of memory today.

2 GIMLET. What!

3 INSPECTOR. Yes. He turned right at Marshall's Corner.

4 GIMLET. What lengths won't they go to get at me!

5 INSPECTOR. I don't know what you're talking about.

6 GIMLET. *They* know, though. *They* know.

GRUNGE *enters right.*

7 GRUNGE. Can't find him.

8 INSPECTOR. He's gone.

9 GRUNGE. Oh, blimey! I ought to get double time on this job. [*He turns to go.*]

10 NELLIE. What about your jam tart?

11 GRUNGE. What jam tart?

12 NELLIE. You ordered jam tart.

13 GRUNGE. That was my mate.

14 NELLIE. It was you.

15 GRUNGE. Then I don't want it.

16 NELLIE. You're not going to let it go to waste!

17 GRUNGE. All right, wrap it up. I'll take it with me.

18 NELLIE. With custard on it?

19 GRUNGE. Oh, I dunno.

GRUNGE *exits right.*

20 GIMLET. Was anyone hurt?

21 INSPECTOR. Nothing serious. Only now, of course, we've got our first open-top double-decker.

The INSPECTOR *exits right.* GIMLET *rises, goes to the pin-table and begins to play.*

22 NELLIE. You'll never win. It's not made so's you can win.

23 GIMLET [*looking at* NELLIE]. Some people could.

IRIS, DOGG'S *conductress, enters right. She carries her handbag.*

1 IRIS [*crossing to centre*]. Hallo, Ernie.

2 GIMLET [*intent on his game*]. You all right?

3 IRIS. You heard about it, then?

4 GIMLET. Yes. [*He turns to* IRIS.] Iris . . .

5 IRIS. What?

6 GIMLET. How's your mother?

7 IRIS. She's all right. [*She sits above the left end of the table right centre.*] I feel a bit weak. D'you think you could get me a cup of tea?

8 GIMLET. Yes, of course. Cup of tea, Nellie.

NELLIE *pours a cup of tea.*

9 NELLIE. With sugar?

10 GIMLET. Lots of sugar. [*He collects the tea from the counter and puts it on the table in front of* IRIS.]

NELLIE *exits behind the counter.*

11 IRIS. Thanks, Ernie.

12 GIMLET. Feeling better now?

13 IRIS. I'm all right.

14 GIMLET. Good. Iris . . .

15 IRIS. What?

16 GIMLET. Will you come to the pictures with me tomorrow night?

IRIS *looks slowly up at him.*

What's wrong?

17 IRIS. Is that all you have to say to me?

18 GIMLET. What do you mean?

19 IRIS. I come in straight from an accident and all you're interested in is whether I can go to the pictures with you.

1 GIMLET. But I don't . . .

2 IRIS. How egotistic can you get?

3 GIMLET. I asked how you were.

4 IRIS. Yes, while you played the pin-table at the same time. You couldn't waste the penny, could you?

5 GIMLET. I had it in my hand when you came in. I just let go, that's all. For goodness' sake, I've been waiting for you over half an hour. I've got to go in a few minutes.

6 IRIS. I'm very sorry. I apologize for being late.

7 GIMLET. What have I *done?*

8 IRIS. Nothing. You haven't done anything. [*She weeps.*]

9 GIMLET. Shock.

10 IRIS. That's right, put it down to shock. That makes it all right, doesn't it?

11 GIMLET. Look, Iris . . .

12 IRIS. Oh, leave me alone. Go back to your pin-table.

> GIMLET *looks at* IRIS *for a few moments, then goes to the pin-table.* BERT DOGG, *a bus driver, enters right. His head is bandaged.*

13 DOGG [*crossing to left centre*]. Well, well, here I am.

14 GIMLET. Dogg . . .

15 DOGG. Hallo, Gimlet, old friend. You still here?

16 GIMLET. I've got five minutes yet. You timed it badly.

17 DOGG [*moving above the pin-table*]. You're not playing that right.

18 GIMLET. Do you mind!

19 DOGG. Never win if you play it fair, you know. Have to jigger it about—like this, see? [*He pushes the machine.*]

20 GIMLET. You've tilted it! You've . . . ! [*He is speechless.*]

21 DOGG. Don't know me own strength, do I? You heard about my little error of judgment, I suppose? Happens to the best of us, that's what I say. [*He moves to* IRIS.] Iris, my pet, you're not looking at all well. How do you feel?

22 IRIS. I'm all right, Bert.

1   DOGG. You shouldn't have bothered to come back. Delayed shock, that's what this is. [*He picks up her cup.*] Here, drink this tea.

DOGG holds the cup while IRIS sips the tea.

2   IRIS. I'm all right, really.

3   DOGG. No, you're not. [*He puts down the cup.*] Tell you what: you just sit there quietly for a few minutes while they sort this out in the office, and then I'll take you home and put you straight to bed. All right?

4   IRIS. If you say so, Bert.

5   DOGG. Not another word, then. Want something to eat?

6   IRIS. I'll wait till I get home.

7   DOGG. Sit quiet, then, while I get things straightened out. Won't be long. [*to GIMLET*] Look after her for a minute, will you, old friend? Here, she might like to look at the paper. [*He takes a newspaper from GIMLET's overcoat pocket and gives it to IRIS.*] Here you are, take your mind off it. Get her another cup of tea if she wants it. And don't make too much noise with that thing, will you? She wants to be quiet.

DOGG crosses and exits right. GIMLET looks at his watch and moves to IRIS.

8   GIMLET. Do you want another cup of tea?

IRIS shakes her head.

Biscuit or . . . ?

9   IRIS. No, thanks.

GIMLET hovers left of IRIS.

You don't have to stay.

10   GIMLET. I won't if you don't want me to.

11   IRIS. I didn't say I didn't want you to.

There is a pause. GIMLET takes out a cigarette and lights it.

I haven't seen you around lately.

1 GIMLET. That's the way it goes, isn't it? You won't see me at all after this week.

2 IRIS. What?

3 GIMLET. I'm getting my cards.

4 IRIS. What's happened?

5 GIMLET. Nothing's happened. I'm just packing the job in.

6 IRIS. Why?

7 GIMLET. Why not? There's nothing in it for me here.

8 IRIS. What are you going to do?

9 GIMLET. Go back to baking, I suppose.

10 IRIS. I thought you didn't like baking.

11 GIMLET. What's that got to do with it?

12 IRIS. If you're not happy in the job . . .

13 GIMLET. Happy! I'm not meant to be happy. I'm not one of the blokes who's supposed to be happy.

14 IRIS. That's a silly way of looking at it.

15 GIMLET. No, all right . . .

16 IRIS. I mean, I don't think it's a very mature attitude.

17 GIMLET. No, well, I'm only a lad, you see. My ambition, of course, is to be a really mature man of the world like Bert Dogg.

18 IRIS. I wasn't thinking of Bert. [*She pauses.*] Well, I hope you get on all right.

19 GIMLET. What?

20 IRIS. Making doughnuts.

21 GIMLET. Thanks very much. [*He pauses.*] You don't like me, do you?

22 IRIS. What makes you say that?

23 GIMLET. It's just suddenly occurred to me.

24 IRIS. I didn't think you were interested in what people thought of you.

25 GIMLET. No, that's right. Hell, hell!

1 IRIS. What's the matter with you, Ernie Gimlet?

2 GIMLET. D'you really want to know? I've just realized. I'm nobody who wants to be somebody, that's all. That's what's the matter with me.

3 IRIS. I don't understand you.

4 GIMLET. Don't bother; it's not worth it.

5 IRIS. I'm washing my hair tomorrow night, anyhow.

6 GIMLET. I thought you probably would be.

7 IRIS. I always wash my hair on a Friday.

8 GIMLET. How interesting!

9 IRIS. What are you angry about?

10 GIMLET. I'm not angry.

11 IRIS. Then don't shout.

12 GIMLET. I'm not angry. I'm just sick of—everything being so ordinary. I'm sick of being—being . . .

There is a pause.

13 IRIS. You don't know what you're sick of, do you? You don't know *what* you want. [*She pauses.*] Everything's wrong for you, isn't it?

14 GIMLET. I've got two minutes. Let's not . . .

15 IRIS. It's all wrong for you. The whole world. You ask whether I like you; how can I like you? When you do nothing but brag and bellyache. The trouble is I'm fond of you. But I don't like you. I suppose you think yourself a mixed-up kid. Well, you're a bit bloody old to be a mixed-up kid.

16 GIMLET. Please don't swear.

17 IRIS. Why shouldn't I?

18 GIMLET. Because it makes you ordinary. Like everyone else. Like me. [*He goes to the pin-table and searches in a distracted way amongst his change for a penny.*]

19 IRIS. Is that it?

20 GIMLET. Leave me alone.

1   IRIS. D'you want a penny? We're all ordinary. What do you expect? Glamour?

LILLIAN enters right.

2   LILLIAN [*crossing to centre*]. Mr. Gimlet—I hate to break into your afternoon, but I thought you might like to know we have a bus full of passengers waiting your convenience, and we're due out in thirty seconds' time.

GIMLET gives LILLIAN a long look.

Don't look at *me*; it's not my fault. Well, are you coming or shall I give your apologies to the passengers? [*She pauses.*] May I have an answer?

3   GIMLET. Miss Fitch, we've been getting on each other's nerves for some months. Even you must have cottoned on to the fact I'm just not *original* enough to walk out on a bus-load of passengers, much as I'd like to. I'm just an ordinary bus driver like all the rest. So why don't you quit pestering me?

4   LILLIAN. We're in agreement at last. I had the idea you considered yourself something exceptional. I'm glad to know you've changed your mind. I shall be on the bus when you decide to come.

LILLIAN exits right.

5   GIMLET. No, not glamour.

6   IRIS. What?

7   GIMLET. I said it wasn't glamour I wanted.

8   IRIS. If you like, I'll put off washing my hair and we'll . . .

9   GIMLET. Go ahead and wash your hair.

10   IRIS. But you wanted to . . .

11   GIMLET. Look, I'm just a bloody misery; I'm immature, see. I shall spend my life wanting things I can't have. You wash your hair; it'll be something accomplished. You won't accomplish anything with me.

12   IRIS. But I don't want to wash my hair, any more.

1   GIMLET. Then go to the pictures with Bert Dogg.

2   IRIS. You're being rather petty.

3   GIMLET. Exactly. You hang on to Bert Dogg. He's a steady bloke. He wants what he's got. He doesn't worry about what he's turning into. He's mature, see?

4   IRIS. I don't *want* to go to the pictures with Bert.

5   GIMLET. Then wash your hair. [*He collects his coat and cap.*] I've got to go. [*He puts on his coat.*]

6   IRIS. What's the *matter* with you? I'm not *tied* to you. I hardly even *know* you. We've only been out *twice* together. And we're acting as though we're . . .

7   GIMLET. Married.

8   IRIS. Hm?

9   GIMLET. Quarrelling as though we're married. [*He pauses.*] You know old Nimrod? [*He points up right.*] Bloke who always sits over there. Cheese sandwiches and a thermos flask. He was my age, once. A young man. Larked about; had ideals. Thought it was just a matter of time before he got what he wanted. He was just waiting for the day. He must have looked at people who were like he is now and said, 'Not for me. I'm for something else than that. I'm going to make life what I want it to be.' But *he's* sitting there now, and I'm looking at him like he used to look at those other blokes. And in twenty years' time *I'll* be sitting there, and there'll be some other young bloke full of life, looking at *me*. 'Oh, no,' he'll say, 'life's not gonna get *me* like that.' And Fran? She was young once. *She* used to go out with her boy-friend with her eyes full of stars and her heart full of . . . Look at her, now. What d'you think happened? You think it was an accident? No—she just *grew* up. That's all. Like all the rest of them, all this shower of misery. You think we'll be any different? You'll be Fran, I'll be Nimrod. Don't you believe me? You think there's a way out? It's all a fraud, you see. Everything we want, everything we're brought up to value, everything we think we can hold in our hands and keep—none of it

lasts, *none* of it. Name me something that lasts! It's all a fraud, don't you get it?

There is a pause.

2   IRIS. But, Ernie . . .

3   GIMLET. See you in twenty years' time.

   GIMLET exits right.

4   IRIS. It's not true. [*She takes out a mirror from her handbag, stares into it and runs one finger along her brow.*]

   NELLIE *enters behind the counter.*

5   NELLIE. Do you want another cup of tea, dear? While it's still hot.

   IRIS *does not reply.*
   DOGG *enters right and crosses to centre.*

6   DOGG. Well, it's all fixed. We've got the rest of the day off. Come on, I'll take you home.

7   IRIS. All right. [*She rises.*] No. [*She pauses.*] Bert.

8   DOGG. What is it?

9   IRIS. I don't want to go home. I'm feeling all right now.

10 DOGG. You sure?

11 IRIS. I'm quite sure. Take me to the pictures, Bert.

12 DOGG. You really think you'll be . . .?

13 IRIS. I've told you, haven't I? Do you want to take me to the pictures or not?

14 DOGG. Come on, then, my pet.

   DOGG *and* IRIS *exit right.* NELLIE *comes from behind the counter and clears the remaining plates, etc.*

15 NELLIE. One thing's certain in this life: no matter what happens—weddings, razor-fights, Lord Mayor's Shows, fires, floods, or just the plain ordinary everyday grind of earning bread and butter—the last thing you'll see, if you wait around long enough, will be some poor bleeder clearing up the mess.

FRAN *enters behind the counter.*

1 FRAN. I never finished telling you what happened.

2 NELLIE. What to?

3 FRAN. Me. Last night. When I saw Sid.

4 NELLIE. Well, what did happen?

5 FRAN. Nothing. I went up to him where he was sitting there with this friend of his, and I said, 'Hallo, Sid', I said. And he never even looked up. He just went on talking to this friend, as though he hadn't heard. As though I wasn't there. [*She pauses briefly.*] I'll give you a hand with them things.

FRAN *comes from behind the counter as the* CURTAIN FALLS.

No Why

by John Whiting

Die Ros' ist ohn' Warum, sie bluhet, weil sie bluhet,
Sie acht't nicht ihrer selbst, fragt nicht, ob man sie siehet.*
ANGELUS SILESIUS

*The rose is without a why, it blossoms because it blossoms,
It has no regard for itself, it asks not whether it is seen.

The scene is an unfurnished attic. It is night.

CHARACTERS

JACOB, a child

HENRY, his father

ELEANOR, his mother

MAX, his cousin

SARAH ⎫
       ⎬ his aunts
AMY   ⎭

GREGORY, his grandfather

TWO SERVANTS

ACTING NOTE

No Why

The roof is beamed. There is no window, and the only light comes from a single unshaded electric lamp. There is one door, up centre. The only furniture is an upright chair placed down right centre. The lamp is on a small wood shelf right. When the curtain rises, a small boy is sitting on the chair. He is in pyjamas. His name is JACOB. *Throughout the play, except when indicated otherwise, he looks in front of him, appearing neither to see nor hear anything which occurs.*

After a moment the door is unlocked from outside. HENRY, JACOB'S *father, enters and comes down to left of the boy.*

1 HENRY. You know why you're here.

> JACOB *appears to be about to speak.*

Shut up. You know why, don't you? Bad boy. I want you to understand. Naughty boy. Say you're sorry. Come on, tell me you're sorry. We all do things we're sorry for. Ask to be forgiven. So much better. For you. For everybody. Makes them happy. Make you happy, too. [*He crosses slowly above the chair to right of it.*] You know you've done a bad thing. A bad thing. Mischief. You've hurt me very much. You've hurt your mother. Yes, your mother, Jake. You've hurt her very much. Make it better, will you? [*He kneels beside* JACOB.] Will you? Say you've done wrong. Look at me, Jake. Say you've been a bad boy.

> ELEANOR, JACOB'S *mother, enters. She cries out.*

2 ELEANOR. No! [*She crosses to left of the chair.*]

3 HENRY. I'm not touching him. [*He gets up.*] I haven't touched him.

4 ELEANOR. Don't hurt him.

5 HENRY. I won't hurt him. I'm being very reasonable. Christ's sake, Eleanor, when have I ever hurt him? I've always been fair. I want him to admit that he's been naughty. Done a bad thing. That's all.

1   ELEANOR [*to* JACOB]. Say you're sorry, Jake. Tell mother you're sorry.

2   HENRY. It's pride. [*He moves away to down right.*]

3   ELEANOR. Not in a little boy.

4   HENRY. Stuffed. Up to here.

5   ELEANOR [*to* JACOB; *kneeling by him*]. Listen Jake. You've done a bad thing. Wicked. No, not wicked.

6   HENRY. Yes, wicked. [*He returns to the boy.*] We had a nice day today, didn't we, Jake? All of us, together. You enjoyed yourself. Yes, you did. I know you did. I saw you laughing. You were happy. Yes, you were. Quite right. We all wanted it to be a good day. One to remember. For grandfather's sake. And it was. A very good day. [*He pauses.*] Until you did such a bad thing. As your mother says, a wicked thing. Well, it's done. Day's spoilt. Nothing can make it good. No, nothing can make it good now. Pity. Nothing. But you can say you're sorry, Jake. Say you're sorry.

Silence.

7   ELEANOR [*rising and moving away to left centre*]. He doesn't understand what he's done. He just doesn't understand.

8   HENRY [*crossing above the chair to right of* ELEANOR]. He may not understand what he's done, but he must understand, I've made it perfectly clear to him, that it was wrong.

9   ELEANOR. It's not enough. You must understand. You must. I know.

10   HENRY. You're a fool.

11   ELEANOR. I want you to explain to him, that's all.

12   HENRY. You want me to pretend. You want me to end up in the wrong. End up by admitting that I'm the one who's done wrong. Have me confess. Have me on my knees. I know you. Anything for a quiet life. A quiet life. That's what you want.

13   ELEANOR. No. I just want you to explain to him.

Silence.

1 HENRY [*returning to left of* JACOB]. Jake, it's easy to go wrong. As you grow up you'll find it's very easy. We can do harm. We can hurt people. But we don't do these things. As you did today. We don't do them because . . . [*He breaks off and pauses.*]

Silence.

[*suddenly shouting*] Who the hell do you think you are!

Silence.

[*more calmly*] Why did you do it? I don't understand. Tell me why you did it.

2 ELEANOR. He doesn't know.

3 HENRY. Well, he knows he's shut up. [*to* JACOB, *crossing above to right of him*] You know that, don't you? You know you're being punished.

4 ELEANOR. We want you to have time to think over what you've done.

5 HENRY. That's right. Because we love you. We love you very much. We want to forgive you. Let's do that. Say you're sorry.

6 ELEANOR. You haven't explained. You haven't.

7 HENRY. I know. You want me down on my knees. To him.

8 ELEANOR. No, I want—

9 HENRY. Have I done wrong? Well, have I? You want me to say so. I know. I know what you want.

10 ELEANOR [*moving to left of* JACOB].—I want him to understand, that's all.

11 HENRY. There are prisons. [*He crouches down by the chair.*] Jake, listen. Men are shut up all over the world. In prisons. Bad men, wicked men. Men who have done harm. As you did today. They sit by themselves. In little rooms. They walk in circles. In yards. Outside—[*pointing to the door*] out there!—are the others. We are the others. We are free. We live good lives. We don't destroy. We're good. We're good, Jake. Those shut up are bad. They're

75

bad, Jake. So bad, some of them, so bad they never get free. They die shut up. Die. Never seen again. No. [*He pauses.*] Say you're sorry, Jake.

Silence. HENRY *rises and moves a pace to right.*

2 ELEANOR. Do you know what I'm thinking about, Jake? [*She smiles.*] I'm thinking about you grown up.

3 HENRY. Have you forgotten what he's done?

4 ELEANOR. No. No.

5 HENRY. Then why are you smiling? Why are you talking about the future?

6 ELEANOR. Because I want him with me. [*She kneels beside the chair.*] I want you with me, Jake. I shall need you. Always. Never away from me. So please your father. Be a good boy.

MAX *enters up centre. He is a young man.*

7 MAX [*moving to left of* HENRY]. Uncle Henry, Mummy wants to know how long you're going to be?

8 HENRY [*taking* MAX's *arm*]. Look, Jake, here's your cousin Max.

9 MAX [*to* ELEANOR]. Mummy says you could be done with this in no time.

ELEANOR *rises.*

10 HENRY. Now you've always liked Max. Or so it seemed. Aren't you disappointed? Max was going to play the piano and sing some songs. And you were going to be allowed down, Jake. You were going to be allowed down to listen. With the grown-ups.

11 MAX [*to* ELEANOR; *moving above the chair to her*]. Fancy. I'd never have got away with it when I was a kid.

12 ELEANOR. He doesn't understand.

13 HENRY. Max will sing some funny songs for us. And you can come down, Jake. When you've said you're sorry. Say you're sorry.

Silence. MAX *squats beside* JACOB, *looking up at him.*

1   MAX. Come on, Jakey boy. Don't spoil the party. Gramp doesn't get much pleasure in life. His fun's over. But you've got it all, boy. If you're good. If you say you're sorry. Because you've got to be good in some things so's you can be bad in others. Follow? Say you're sorry, you bad lad. Then everything's in front of you. See? Let Max teach you. If you knew what it's all about you wouldn't want to throw it away like this. Come on, you want to grow up, don't you? Then say: I'm sorry.

Silence.

2   HENRY. He doesn't care.

3   MAX. Who does? Let's be honest.

4   HENRY. He must be made to care.

5   MAX. Up to you. [*He rises and moves above* ELEANOR *to up left.*]

6   HENRY [*to* JACOB]. You can't win! Not now! Save what you can, you little fool!

Silence.

[*loudly; moving in to* JACOB] I'll put you through hell!

Silence.

7   ELEANOR [*kneeling left of the chair*]. Remember when you were a little boy.

8   HENRY. That's it. Remember how I taught you your prayers?

MAX *moves down left.*

9   ELEANOR. You remember how they go.

10   HENRY. Of course you do.

11   ELEANOR [*to* HENRY]. Oh, darling, I'm so happy.

12   HENRY [*crouching down*]. Let's try it, Jake. Just a little one to please me. I'll give you a start. Gentle Jesus, meek and mild. Go on from there. [*He waits.*] Well, anyway, you once said them. You said them once. I remember, if you don't. Down on your knees. Now look at you. Look at you now. Breaking a promise to Jesus, that's what you're

doing. [*He rises.*] Think of it, Jake. Oh, Jake! To Jesus. How can you do it? How can you?

Silence. SARAH *enters up centre and moves down to right of* MAX.

2 MAX. Mammy, Jake's being such a naughty boy. Won't say he's sorry for dreadful things he's done. He's damned, sure enough. His daddy promised him to come downstairs and hear me sing and play if he'll confess. But no, he's mum, Mammy. Oh, he's damned.

3 SARAH [*putting her hand on* MAX'S *arm*]. You're a good boy, Max. You never disobeyed your father. When he was alive.

4 MAX. Oh, Mammy, I loved Daddy with all my heart.

5 HENRY. This child loves no one. [*He moves away down right.*]

6 ELEANOR. He loves me!

7 HENRY [*turning*]. You?

8 ELEANOR. He loves me!

9 HENRY [*to* JACOB]. Do you?

10 ELEANOR. Yes.

11 HENRY [*to* JACOB]. Love your mother?

Silence. HENRY *laughs.*

12 ELEANOR. It doesn't need to be said. [*She rises and moves above the chair.*]

13 HENRY. Which is lucky for you. It never will be.

14 SARAH [*moving a pace to centre*]. Ah, this child doesn't understand the beauty of love. Pretty pretty. Doesn't understand the pleasure of giving in. I knew it so well! Until my hubbie was taken from me. To wake and find no one to submit to was a terrible thing.

15 MAX. You've still got me, Mammy.

16 SARAH [*moving back to* MAX]. Yes, darling, I've still got you. [*She fondles him in a disgusting way.*]

17 MAX. Oo, Mammy, I love you, I love you so.

18 HENRY [*to* JACOB]. See that, Jake? Hear that? Ashamed of yourself?

1   SARAH. Darling.

2   MAX. Oo.

3   SARAH. Sweet.

4   MAX. Oo.

5   SARAH. Kisskiss.

6   MAX. Oo, lovee.

MAX *and* SARAH *kiss.* HENRY *looks down at* JACOB.

7   HENRY. I had hopes of you. Even from the start. It was all so
romantic. Soft lights and sweet music. Dancing cheek
to cheek. I was young. When I think of that I could cry.
True, I could cry. [*He moves to* ELEANOR *above the chair,
groping for her hand. To her*] Remember how we planned for
him? What should he be like, our son? Should he walk
on two legs or on four? We decided two, remember?
So his head should be nearer the clouds. You wanted
that with your love of pansy poetry. The more feet on
the ground the more realistic his outlook, I thought.
But you kissed me and I gave in. And he turned out just
as our conception of him. All seemed right. Remember
how happy we were? Remember the long winter even-
ings as we sat reading the school year-book and careers
for boys and he lay farting in his cot? And we laughed
and loved him so much. [*He stares down at* JACOB.] That was
this little criminal.

8   ELEANOR. You forget. You exaggerate. We had him in the
same way everyone has their boy. More or less. It was
late. You were tired. I was nearly asleep. There was
nothing strange or wonderful about it. Of course we
talked about his school when he was little, and what he
might be when he grew up. But only because you worry
about money so much. It was all from the very start for
our sake, not for his.

HENRY *lets go of* ELEANOR'S *hand, and moves away right.*

9   HENRY. You're taking his part again. This is not the time. If I
was as soft as you are you'd have broken my heart long
ago. Stand up to the boy!

1 ELEANOR [*to* JACOB; *standing above the chair*]. Are you sorry for what you've done?

2 HENRY [*to* ELEANOR]. Are you?

Silence. ELEANOR *turns slightly up stage.*

3 MAX. Mammy, when I was little was I sweet?

4 SARAH. You were adorable.

5 MAX. Did you ever have to shut me up like this?

6 SARAH. Never.

7 MAX. Not ever?

8 SARAH. No.

9 MAX. Did you ever have to give me a little smack?

10 SARAH [*after a pause*]. Once.

11 MAX. Oo, Mammy!

AMY *enters and comes down centre.*

12 AMY. I've had to leave Father down there. It doesn't seem right.

13 MAX [*crossing below* SARAH *to* AMY]. Does he want to come up?

JACOB *looks at* AMY.

14 AMY. Well, you know what he's like. Hates to miss any fun that may be going. But I can't get the wheelchair up the stairs.

15 MAX [*moving up centre*]. I love Gramp very much. I won't let him be lonely. I won't.

MAX *goes out.*

16 SARAH. That's right, Jake. Look at your Aunt Amy. She's a really good woman.

ELEANOR, *above the chair, turns downstage again.* JACOB *looks out front.*

17 AMY. No, Sarah.

18 SARAH. Yes, Amy. A good woman.

1   AMY. No, Sarah, like little Jake here, I'm a wicked sinner. But I repent. Every time.

2   SARAH [*putting her hand on* AMY'S *arm*]. Oh, you serene and beautiful person. You're wonderful, like—like treacle.

3   AMY. Has he said he's sorry yet?

4   HENRY. No.

5   AMY. Perhaps I can help. [*She kneels left of the chair.*] When I was a little girl, Jake, about your age, I wanted everything in the world for myself. I thought I was beautiful——

6   SARAH. You were, Amy.

7   AMY. —talented——

8   SARAH. You were.

9   AMY. —and lovable.

10 SARAH. Wasn't she, Henry?

11 AMY. And I thought I had a right to everything. I was lost in a dream——

12 SARAH. Cut it short, Amy. Get to the point. Tell him about your prison visiting. How you tramp the hospital wards. And how you love the lunatics.

13 AMY. I go to see the prisoners, Jake. Sometimes the condemned men. They often take my hand and ask forgiveness. As you can. Now. Will you?

Silence. JACOB *does not move.*

I go into the hospital wards. No sudden death there. A florid growth back to nature. There's a man who is nothing but an enormous mouth, and he always asks my blessing. Will you? [*She pauses.*] In the asylums they run to me. Their darling childish faces are shining with love. Their trust is so great. One night a young girl lay still. Moths settled on her open eyes and drowned there. The insane can learn nothing from me of faith and serenity. But will you?

Silence.

1 HENRY. Don't you understand what your Aunt Amy gave up to bring comfort to all these people? Haven't you any respect? She's offering her love to you and you won't accept it.

2 AMY. It doesn't matter, Henry. [*She rises.*]

3 HENRY. It does matter, Amy. Is he so proud that he thinks himself better than the condemned, the sick and the mad? At least he should recognize the sacrifices you've made. Oh, Amy, you were such a lovely girl when we were children. Has it been worth it? Living your life for others?

4 AMY. Always, Henry, when others accept it. Not like this bloody little bastard of yours. This filth.

5 SARAH. I don't know how you and Eleanor came to have such a child. How does our lovely, adorable brother come to have such a child, Amy?

6 AMY. Perhaps as a curse.

7 SARAH. From God, darling? They come from God, you know.

8 AMY. Of course, Henry, there is the criminal who doesn't repent. The sick man who dies in silence. The madman who laughs and turns away. Some don't need others. To hell with them! [*She moves away up left.*]

9 HENRY [*He kneels in front of* JACOB.] Say you're sorry. I'll do anything. I'll give you anything. Jacob. Listen. You heard what Amy said. Come back to the family party before it's too late. Come with me. Please. Darling. Come back. Come back.

Silence. ELEANOR *cries out and moves away a pace up stage. A long silence.*

Come back.

Two SERVANTS *enter. They carry* GREGORY, JACOB'S *grandfather, on a kitchen chair. He is old, a thrown-away doll of a man. The* SERVANTS *set him down centre, facing the child.* MAX *has followed them into the room.*

82

1 MAX. Just as you said. He couldn't bear to miss the fun. [*He crosses above Sarah to down left of her.*]

2 SARAH. Father! Jake won't say he's sorry.

3 GREGORY. Does it matter?

The SERVANTS *stand up centre.*

4 ELEANOR. What do you mean? Doesn't it matter? Needn't he say it? Can he come down without saying it?

5 GREGORY. No. It doesn't matter because it's too late.

6 ELEANOR. Too late?

7 GREGORY. Yes. If all criminals got away with saying they're sorry, where should we be?

JACOB *looks at* GREGORY.

8 ELEANOR. He doesn't understand what he's done.

9 GREGORY. Nobody understands what they do. You sound as if you think that's an excuse. You're a fool. You always were a fool.

10 HENRY. So I tell her, Father.

11 ELEANOR [*to* GREGORY]. Please try and make him say he's sorry.

GREGORY *and* JACOB *stare at each other.*

12 GREGORY. Why should I? It doesn't matter now. Not when you get to my age. It's not important, I tell you. All that matters is something called—[*He hesitates.*] justice.

JACOB *looks out front again.*

13 MAX [*to* SARAH]. Oh, he's right. That matters lots. Where'd we be without it?

14 GREGORY. Has anybody got anything good to say about the boy? No matter how insignificant. Come on, speak up.

15 ELEANOR. He's always been very sweet to me. Loved me very much.

16 MAX [*as if declaiming newspaper headlines*]. 'Mother's love fails to save child.'

1 AMY [*coming down to above left of* GREGORY's *chair.*] They all love their mother. They cling to the idea. On the scaffold, under the knife. I love Mummy.

2 GREGORY. Remorse. Any sign of it?

3 HENRY. I'm afraid not. After discovering the crime I went to see him. He was sitting up in bed eating jelly and drinking milk.

4 GREGORY. Seemed unconcerned?

5 HENRY. Yes.

6 MAX. 'Distressing scene. Father in box. Admits son's guilt.'

7 GREGORY. Has he been in trouble before?

8 HENRY. He used to wet his bed. He's over it now.

9 MAX. 'Medical evidence causes stir.'

10 GREGORY. Let's come to the actual crime. Sarah, did you see it?

11 SARAH. Certainly not. I wouldn't look. I'm not used to such things. Ask Max. I always keep things nice.

12 MAX. She does, Gramp.

13 SARAH. I keep off the nasty. So I wouldn't look at what Jake did.

14 ELEANOR. Then how did you know it was so bad?

15 SARAH [*shouting*]. I read the newspapers, don't I? I know what a man is! [*She points at* JACOB.] That! It ought not to be allowed!

MAX *protects her, putting his arm round her.*

16 GREGORY. Amy, you're used to everything. The whole bag of tricks. Lunacy, sickness, the lot. What's your opinion? How bad was this?

17 AMY [*left of* GREGORY's *chair*]. It was unforgivable. In my experience. A crime. An atrocity.

18 GREGORY [*to* JACOB]. You hear that? What do you expect us to do? Take you back as our little boy? Our hope and our future. You can't expect that.

1   MAX. 'Judge sums up.'

2   HENRY. I've tried to explain to him how we live, Father.

3   GREGORY. Does he understand?

4   HENRY. I think he understands that the road back is long and hard.

5   GREGORY. I'm too old to go back, Henry.

6   HENRY [*gently*]. We're talking about Jacob, Father.

7   GREGORY. Little Jacob. What's he done?

8   AMY [*shortly*]. He exists, Father. Look at him, there in front of your face. He is, Father.

   GREGORY *turns and stares at the child.*

9   GREGORY [*laughing loudly*]. Jesus Christ. I don't have to find any punishment for you. Take me away.

10   MAX. 'Sensation. Child condemned.'

11   GREGORY. Take me away.

   The two SERVANTS *lift* GREGORY *in his chair.* AMY *moves up left centre.*

12   SARAH. You will let Max sing his song, won't you? The one about the commercial traveller's mother-in-law. He's learnt it specially.

13   GREGORY. Yes, let Max sing his song.

14   MAX. Oo, thank you, Gramp.

15   SARAH [*turning to* MAX]. If I get a bit tiddly, Max, promise to tuck me up, sweet.

16   MAX. 'Course, Mummeee.

   The SERVANTS *carry* GREGORY *from the room.* SARAH *and* AMY *exit after them.* MAX *moves up to the door.*

17   ELEANOR [*to* HENRY]. Let me stay with him.

18   HENRY. No.

19   MAX. 'Last appeal fails.'

   MAX *goes out.* ELEANOR *follows him, shutting the door.* HENRY *and* JACOB *are left alone.*

1   HENRY. When all's said and done there are only two left face to face. The executioner and the victim. And when it comes to that, Jake, when it comes to us, left alone, together, like this, what is there between us? [*He moves slowly above the chair and round to centre.*] There's no hate. There's no love. There's nothing. Because we recognize each other for what we are. But the executioner comes out of the shed alive. Unfair. Poor devil.

Silence. When HENRY *speaks again, a second voice is heard. It is* HENRY'S, *amplified and independent. It speaks the following words.* HENRY *also speaks these words, and he is aware of the voice. Glancing about, he tries to shout it down. He hesitates, falters, catches up again to speak in unison, is borne inexorably along until the last moment.*

It has to be this way. Because we are good. Out there. [*He indicates the door.*] Good people. Living good lives. We've repented our existence. We're truly sorry that we are. We're on our knees for being. So we're allowed to go free. We're allowed to go wherever we like all over this little, tiny world. We're not confined. Oh, no. [*He moves down left.*] First of all there's the secure freedom of the womb. There's the freedom of the family. The freedom of loving someone. And more, being loved. And at the end there's the liberty of the tomb. [*returning to centre*] All this could have been yours, Jake, if you'd said you were sorry. Don't you see what you were being offered? How could you be so stubborn? You were being offered what everybody wants. And you refused.

Silence. The second voice begins. HENRY *stumbles after it.*

You brought it on yourself. Look at us now. No feeling, as there should be between father and son. Not even feeling as between two human beings. You in here. And I'm . . .

2   HENRY'S VOICE [*alone*]. Out here.

3   HENRY. You did it. You did it. First. By the enormity of your crime. Second. By refusing to confess. Confess. You did

it. You did it. I wanted to love you so much. I wanted us to be together. I wanted to love you. Now . . .

2   HENRY'S VOICE. I wish you'd never been born!

3   HENRY. No!

4   HENRY'S VOICE. I wish you'd never been born!

5   HENRY [*in a whisper*]. I wish you'd never been born!

Silence. A piano begins to play below: a popular tune. There is the sound of laughter.

[*alone*] I'm going down, now. [*He moves above the chair to the shelf right.*] I'm going back to the party. You'll stay up here tonight. You've been a very naughty boy, Jake. You must be punished. I'll come up in the morning. And then I shall hope to find my real little boy. [*He unplugs the electric lamp and moves with it to the door.*] The boy I want to love.

HENRY *goes out. The door is locked. The piano is being played downstairs.* JACOB *gets up from the chair. He comes forward and stares into the theatre. He waits, as if for a word. Do any of us speak? No. And if we did, what would we say?* JACOB *turns and goes up stage into the darkness. The piano plays. The chair falls.*
We get used to the darkness. We see. The CHILD *has hanged himself from one of the roof-beams. He swings on the cord of his pyjamas, and the trousers have fallen about his ankles. He looks a useless object: a bag of bones. Cheap meat on a butcher's hook.*
The piano and the laughter continue, as the CURTAIN FALLS.

See the Pretty Lights

by Alan Plater

The scene is the end of the pier at a rather tatty seaside resort.

CHARACTERS

NORMAN

ENID

ACTING NOTE

※ ※ ※
See the Pretty Lights

As the play opens we hear faintly the sound of the sea and music from the pier pavilion dance hall—either straight dance music or some current pop.

NORMAN *enters. He is thirty, dressed in conservative clothes, has the pallor and bearing of one who lives with office desks and is aware of his near middle-class status. From time to time he smokes a pipe badly.*

He leans on the telescope, takes half a dozen postcards from his pocket, flips through them. Thrusts them back into his pocket, turns and looks through the telescope. He moves into a brief fantasy of the sea.

1 NORMAN. Up periscope . . . right . . . fire, number one! [*watches to see how it goes*] Bad luck, chaps . . . Fire, number two! . . . Come on, come on, number two! . . . what's going on?

    The stage is flooded with light as the illuminations are switched on, and we see ENID, *sitting nearby staring at* NORMAN. *He turns, reacting to the lights and sees her.*

2 ENID. The elastic must have broke.

3 NORMAN. What? Oh no, just . . .

4 ENID. Just the lights, the illuminations . . .

5 NORMAN. Just . . . having a look at the sea.

6 ENID. Oh aye, the sea.

    ENID *has a look at the sea, half-heartedly. She is nineteen, plain, with an aggressive manner—almost coarse at times—and underneath it an air of apathetic resignation.*

7 NORMAN. Just checking up on it.

8 ENID [*bluntly*]. It's still there.

9 NORMAN. Yes, it is, isn't it? It's rather, well, it seems very . . .

10 ENID. Wet.

11 NORMAN. Yes, that's a good word for it.

    He has another look through the telescope.

Wet. You might well say wet.

NORMAN *shrugs.* ENID *gets up and starts to walk away.*

[*hastily*] Are you on holiday?

2 ENID. You what?

3 NORMAN [*more quietly*]. Are you on holiday?

4 ENID [*sharp*]. What do you think?

5 NORMAN. I think you're probably . . . on holiday.

6 ENID. Brilliant! You ought to get a job on telly solving mysteries.

7 NORMAN [*casual*]. Having a nice time?

8 ENID. I'm at the dance, I like dancing.

9 NORMAN [*feeling the night*]. It's grim here in the winter.

10 ENID [*shocked*]. You *live* here?

11 NORMAN. I'm on holiday. I come every year, just on holiday.

12 ENID [*hint of sarcasm*]. Fancy.

> *Pause*
> ENID *wonders about walking away again and has half decided to do so when* NORMAN *speaks again.*

13 NORMAN. Every year since . . . now then, nineteen fifty . . . [*thinks*].

14 ENID. We come a lot.

15 NORMAN [*to himself*]. Fifty one, that was the Festival so . . .

16 ENID. I come with Jean, my friend, you'd like Jean.

17 NORMAN [*responding*]. Do you enjoy coming here?

18 ENID [*shrugs, apathetic*]. It's somewhere to come. Must be grim in the winter.

19 NORMAN. I quite like it. [*slightly pompous*] They cater for *real* holiday-makers, not just for the trippers . . .

20 ENID. We came to see the illuminations. . . . On a coach trip, go back at midnight. Fifteen bob including high tea. From the works. To see the illuminations.

NORMAN realizes his faux pas. But ENID doesn't seem to have heard him. She is at the rail watching the lights.

They're not all that good, are they?

2   NORMAN. Not really my province, illuminations . . .

3   ENID. Hey look at that, there's Ringo . . .

4   NORMAN. Snow White and the Seven Dwarfs . . .

5   ENID. The Queen Mother . . .

6   NORMAN. The flags of the Commonwealth . . .

7   ENID. Elsie Tanner and Miss Nugent . . .

8   NORMAN. Sandringham Lodge . . .

9   ENID. And Sooty . . .

10   NORMAN. Dr. N'Krumah . . .

11   ENID. Who?

12   NORMAN. Dr. N'Krumah . . .

13   ENID. Where?

14   NORMAN. Over there . . . between Westminster Abbey and Tommy Cooper . . .

15   ENID. Cassius Clay . . .

16   NORMAN. Surely it's N'Krumah . . .

17   ENID. Flipping surely it's Cassius Clay . . . your feller doesn't wear boxing gloves . . .

18   NORMAN. He isn't it's just some of the lights have failed. Wait a minute though [*slight condescension*] perhaps you're right.

19   ENID. Course I'm right . . . [*also condescending*] It's not very good of him though.

NORMAN shrugs.

I'm at the dance, I like dancing.

20   NORMAN. I can hear the music.

The music drifts in and out throughout the action—sometimes seven-piece palais with interludes of Top Twenty records.
ENID moves to the shelter and sits down.

93

1 ENID. It was too hot so I came out for some fresh air. I like dancing though.

2 NORMAN [*worldly*]. I'm easy. Dancing. I can take it or I can leave it.

3 ENID. It's a good way of meeting people. I met this poet last year, he *said* he was a poet. He was a student really, working on the Dodgems. He could have been a poet as well, though, couldn't he?

4 NORMAN. Nick Wainwright and his Monarchs of Melody, featuring Eddie and the Tearaways and your Pop Twenty on records . . .

5 ENID. I mean, anybody can be a poet, can't they? You can set up as a poet just like that . . . that's if you want to. I don't bother myself, not a lot . . .

6 NORMAN. I had thought of popping in at the dance myself . . .

Pause.

7 ENID [*surprised*]. You?

8 NORMAN [*casual*]. Later on. Just pop in . . . for a look round.

9 ENID. Fancy. [*She finds the thought strange.*]

10 NORMAN. But it gets so crowded and hot.

11 ENID [*flatly*]. It's with all those people being there.

12 NORMAN. Quieter out here.

13 ENID. That's 'cause there's nobody here. It makes it quiet.

14 NORMAN. Anyway, I've got this card to post.

15 ENID. There isn't a box.

16 NORMAN. I'll post it on the way back to . . . on the way back.

17 ENID. Good idea. [*slight pause*] Seeing as there isn't a box.

Pause.

You *could* pelt it in the sea.

Pause. NORMAN *stares at her.*

In the sea.

18 NORMAN. The sea?

1 ENID. Shipwrecked sailors. They put letters in a bottle and that ...

2 NORMAN. A bottle ...

He looks round, quickly, vaguely, for a bottle, then half smiles but too late to save her joke. He takes out the postcards from his pocket and spreads them out and holds them like a deck of cards. ENID *stares. There are six cards.*

3 ENID. All them?

4 NORMAN. They like to get one every day.

5 ENID. Do they? [*implying something strange about 'they'*].

6 NORMAN. My mother really. So I do them as soon as I get here, then I don't have to remember ...

7 ENID. Heck!

8 NORMAN. Just to post one, every day, that's all, they're all written ready.

9 ENID. I never send any. Never know anything to put.

10 NORMAN [*reading cards one at a time*]. Dear all, arrived safely, had dinner on the train after all, all right, but pricey, love Norman. Dear all, settling in O.K., new landlady, room overlooking bandstand, marked with a cross, food O.K. and plenty of it, love, Norman. Dear all, went to see Spa Follies, follies is the right word but the hypnotist was good, he stood on this chap, I'll tell you about it, love, Norman. Dear all, there's a man staying here from Gateshead, he says Uncle George *didn't* so who *do* you believe ... [*after thought*] still having nice time, weather O.K., love, Norman. ...

He reaches the end of the cards. Looks at her uncertainly.

11 ENID. My mam says don't bother to write, if you get run over or drowned we'll hear soon enough ...

12 NORMAN. It's a bit of a nuisance really.

13 ENID. 'Course, there's eight of us. It's hard to keep track who's away any road.

1 NORMAN. I'm the only one.

Pause.

2 ENID [*casual*]. If it keeps your mother happy.

Pause. NORMAN *looks at his cards pensively.*

3 NORMAN. I'm having a marvellous time.

4 ENID. That's all right, then.

5 NORMAN. Best holiday I've ever had. It says on Friday's . . .

6 ENID [*dead pan*]. I'm glad.

Pause.

How do you know?

7 NORMAN. How do I know what?

8 ENID. When you haven't had it yet? I mean, how do you know? Before you've had it?

9 NORMAN. I just know.

10 ENID. Dead clever, isn't it?

11 NORMAN. I can tell you weeks in advance what sort of a time I'll have.

Pause.

[*semi-soliloquy*] When I'm sitting in the train, I know it. I know it . . . I know it'll be terrible. By about Tuesday I'll have been everywhere, seen the shows, looked at the beach, had my photograph taken . . . all the things I did last year. . . . [*pause*] Makes it easier, you see, I can put anything I like on the postcards . . . nothing's going to happen. I'll be glad when it's over.

Pause.

12 ENID [*baffled*]. What you come for?

13 NORMAN. It's my holiday.

14 ENID. What you come for, if it's lousy?

1   NORMAN. You need the change, you know, a break from the routine. Routine in the office, it drives you mad. Nine o'clock you get there, read the paper, have tea, answer the mail, talk about last night's telly, go for dinner, read the early edition, have tea, answer the afternoon mail, talk about the next lot of telly, go home. . . . [*pause*] Watch telly. It's terrible.

2   ENID [*sympathetic for the first time*]. What you come here for?

3   NORMAN. This . . . this is terrible in a different sort of way. You need the change . . .

     NORMAN *moves to the telescope.*

     [*to himself*] Break in routine. [*at telescope*] I suppose it sounds silly . . .

4   ENID [*puzzled*]. You what?

5   NORMAN. *Silly* . . . I suppose it sounds silly.

6   ENID. No.

     He looks at her.

     It isn't silly.

     Pause.

     The reason it's lousy . . . [*quietly*] it's because you're by yourself.

7   NORMAN [*quietly*]. Yes. . . .

     Pause.

8   ENID [*quickly*]. Course I'm with Jean, my friend, you'd like Jean.

9   NORMAN. I used to have a friend, I used to have three. Arnold, Ernie and Spike. Three.

10   ENID. I always go dancing with Jean. It's a good way to meet people.

11   NORMAN [*slight bitterness*]. Three friends.

12   ENID [*very casual*]. What happened? They get married?

1 NORMAN. How do you know?

2 ENID. Blokes of your age, they're usually married.

3 NORMAN [*taken aback*]. What do you mean? My age?

4 ENID. Well, you must be thirty.

5 NORMAN. And ten months.

6 ENID. Bit late, isn't it?

   Pause.

   I thought it was a bit funny when you said you might
   go to the dance.

7 NORMAN [*stung*]. Why shouldn't I go to the dance?

8 ENID [*shrugs*]. It's a free country, but . . .

9 NORMAN. Well then! How old are you?

10 ENID. I'm nineteen and mind your own business!

   Pause.

11 NORMAN. Arnold, he got married first. Didn't have to, fell in
   love, I suppose. [*slight sourness*] Ernie, he emigrated,
   started a new life in Australia. He was having trouble
   with the old one. Then Spike went to do his National
   Service and this Empire Loyalist sold him a ninety-nine
   year lease.

12 ENID [*blank*]. You what?

13 NORMAN. Gets a clean bed, three meals a day, change of
   underpants. If he behaves himself he gets full remission.
   He'll be out when he's sixty-five. He'd buy anything, old
   Spike, once got an air rifle, the barrel was bent, nearly
   shot himself.

14 ENID. Did he get married?

15 NORMAN. Two years ago. He had to, in the circumstances.

16 ENID. Oh, was there some circumstances?

17 NORMAN. Only one, they thought there might have been
   two. I was reading some statistics, did you know one in
   four marriages under the age of twenty is . . .?

18 ENID [*breaking in*]. Don't be mucky.

NORMAN *shrugs. He looks through the telescope.*

1 NORMAN. It doesn't change much. Still wet.

Pause.

You'll be wanting to get back to the dance.

2 ENID. Doesn't matter.

3 NORMAN. If you want to, just go . . .

4 ENID. I can please myself, can't I?

5 NORMAN. Just carry on. I might pop in later . . .

6 ENID [*sharp*]. I can please myself, can't I?

7 NORMAN [*indifferent*]. Up to you.

Pause. NORMAN *sighs.*

8 ENID. Why didn't you get married?

9 NORMAN. Me?

10 ENID. You're not like . . . or anything, are you?

11 NORMAN [*slowly*]. The trouble is, I'm not properly chartered.

12 ENID [*baffled*]. You're not what?

13 NORMAN. Properly chartered.

14 ENID [*vague*]. Oh.

Pause.

What you talking about?

15 NORMAN. When I left school. I got this job, and my father said stick your toes in, go to night school, get yourself qualified. Get yourself properly chartered then you'll have security. My father said.

16 ENID. Good thing to have. Security.

17 NORMAN. My boss said the same. [*mimics*] We can't have unqualified chaps going to deal with these chaps in Brussels . . . that's when he's looking ahead, you see, Brussels . . . nobody told him we're not joining.*

* Norman refers to the European Common Market.

1 ENID. Security's very good. You need it if you're getting married.

2 NORMAN. Night school, Tuesdays, Thursdays, alternate Fridays, homework the other nights, all to get properly chartered . . .

3 ENID. I did shorthand for a bit, that was Wednesdays though.

4 NORMAN. By the time I was twenty-four I was a third chartered. When I was twenty-seven I was half chartered. Last year I got to be three-quarters chartered. I passed this examination. So I went to the boss. I asked him how much more money I'd get when I was properly chartered, hundred per cent. [*boss voice.*] Paper qualifications. . . ? Doesn't matter, old chap. What we want is experience, know-how. . . .

5 ENID [*concentrating hard*]. You mean . . . you'd wasted all that time passing exams . . . for nothing?

6 NORMAN. I'm staying three-quarters chartered till the day I die. I'll knock at heaven's gate and say it's me, three-quarters chartered, does it make any difference.

Pause.

[*more casual*] Went to see the boss last week . . . just before I came away.

7 ENID. Oh aye.

8 NORMAN. Asked him about a partnership . . . just a junior partnership, that's all.

9 ENID. You need the security.

10 NORMAN. He wouldn't give me one. Fourteen years I've been there but . . .

11 ENID. The rotten devil! What for?

12 NORMAN. Can't have a partnership unless you're properly chartered. . . .

Pause

13 ENID [*lost*]. I don't understand.

1   NORMAN [*earnest*]. Well, you see, I'm not properly chartered ...

2   ENID [*breaking in sharply*]. I know, you've told me about fifty
    flipping times.

    Pause.

3   NORMAN. Well, you did ask ...

4   ENID. What?

5   NORMAN. You wanted to know why I wasn't married ...

6   ENID. Why aren't you?

7   NORMAN. I'm not properly ch ... [*sighs*] I don't know ...

    Pause. Music drifts across.

8   ENID. Dancing, that's a good way of meeting people. I met
    this test pilot, he was going to India next day ... on a
    bus. He had big ears but he was nice.

9   NORMAN. Good. I'm very pleased.

    Pause.

10 ENID. You ought to hand your notice in, them treating you
    like that.

11 NORMAN. You mean leave?

12 ENID. Set up on your own.

13 NORMAN. Set up on my ...

14 ENID. Our Terry did, in his front room, he's a joiner. ...

15 NORMAN. Be independent. ...

    NORMAN *sits down.*

    Hello, city desk ... yes, put them through ...

    ENID *sits down beside him. Hands him imaginary telephone.*

    [*puzzled*] What's this?

16 ENID. New York on the line ...

17 NORMAN. They'll have to wait; I'm talking to Buenos Aires ...

18 ENID. Hold on, New York, do you mind?

1 NORMAN. You'll just have to find somebody that does talk English . . .

2 ENID. Hello. . . . [*to* NORMAN] Moscow, on the other line. . . .

3 NORMAN. Moscow.

4 ENID. Some feller called Smersh, didn't say his first name.

5 NORMAN. I know him . . . now then, Frank, how are you?

6 ENID. I told you it was easy.

7 NORMAN. What?

8 ENID. Setting up on your own.

9 NORMAN. Be your own boss, oh I know. You can have a bath on Wednesday afternoon.

10 ENID. Go to pictures first house.

11 NORMAN. Out of town on business, would you like to leave a message?

12 ENID. That's what our Terry did, he's a joiner.

13 NORMAN. Telephones, different colour for each Continent.

14 ENID. In his front room.

15 NORMAN [*down to earth*]. My father uses the front room for his model railway.

16 ENID. His model railway?

NORMAN *nods. Pause.*

Heck.

17 NORMAN. He's secretary of the society.

18 ENID. Heck.

Pause.

19 NORMAN. He's busy with a new flyover . . . and underpass . . .

Pause.

So it's out of the question, setting up on my own.

20 ENID. Well, you're not properly chartered, are you?

21 NORMAN. I'm three-quarters chartered . . . [*morose*] I'm three-quarters most things.

NORMAN *looks out to sea.*

I'd like to be four-quarters something. [*flicker of smile*] I could run away to sea.

2 ENID. Can you swim?

3 NORMAN. They give you a boat.

4 ENID. It's still wet.

NORMAN *checks through telescope.*

5 NORMAN. Still wet.

Pause.

6 ENID. You'd never think it to look at you.

7 NORMAN. You'll be wanting to get back. . . .

8 ENID. Three-quarters chartered. Your Dad plays trains, pockets full of postcards. . . .

9 NORMAN. The trouble is . . . doesn't matter. You're missing the dance. . . .

10 ENID. I don't mind, if you want to tell me . . . what the trouble is. . . .

Pause.

11 NORMAN. You listen to what people tell you then after a bit you realize it all cancels out . . . when it's too late.

12 ENID. You shouldn't listen.

13 NORMAN. Opposite the office there's some posters.

14 ENID [*vague*]. Posters?

15 NORMAN. There's one poster, it says 'Join the Modern Army' and next to it there's a church one that says 'Thou shalt not kill'. . . .

16 ENID. I don't look at posters.

17 NORMAN. Then one day last year somebody asked me a question and I said 'Yes'. I could have said 'No', but I said 'Yes'. I broke my leg.

18 ENID. What did he ask you?

1 NORMAN. Would you like a game of football on Sunday?

2 ENID. Are you better now?

3 NORMAN. I still limp a bit on cold days.

Pause.

Gasworks.

Pause.

Church League.

Pause.

Division Two.

Pause.

Through saying 'Yes'.

4 ENID. I don't know what you're talking about.

5 NORMAN. That makes two of us.

6 ENID [*maternal*]. You're just lonely, you want to get yourself out more.

7 NORMAN [*slight sarcasm*]. If you say so, Grandma.

8 ENID [*not noticing*]. I know what it's like, mind.

9 NORMAN. Yes, but *you* can always go dancing. I'm too old to go dancing.

10 ENID. I once met this lad, he was … [*precisely*] Northern Area Bantamweight champion … at boxing. And he was real quiet, when he spoke.

11 NORMAN. If you don't get back soon you won't meet anybody.

12 ENID. Just his nose was a bit puffy but it's to be expected really.

13 NORMAN. The heavyweight champion might be there and you're missing him.

14 ENID. It's all right.

Pause. NORMAN *looks at his watch.*

If you're fed up just go home; I'll be all right.

2 NORMAN. You must have missed a lot of dances, while you've been out here.

3 ENID. You just carry on, don't bother about me. Don't forget your postcard, Monday's, for your mother . . .

4 NORMAN. Nick Wainwright, his Monarchs of Melody, Eddie and the Tearaways, your Pop Twenty . . .

5 ENID [sharp]. I'm not going back to the dance!

6 NORMAN. Not going back?

7 ENID. Do you mind?

8 NORMAN [puzzled]. No, it's just . . . you said . . .

9 ENID. I'm not going back!

10 NORMAN. If that's the way you feel . . .

Pause.

[quietly] It's a good way of meeting people.

11 ENID. I hate dances. If I never went to another dance I'd . . . I hate them.

Pause.

12 NORMAN. You said you like dances.

13 ENID [sullen]. Just 'cause you say a thing it doesn't have to be true.

14 NORMAN. I didn't mean to . . .

15 ENID. I can hate dances if I like. Don't need your permission.

16 NORMAN. I quite agree.

17 ENID. It's a free country.

18 NORMAN. That's what they say.

19 ENID. I hate dances.

20 NORMAN. What's wrong with dances?

Pause. ENID clams up.

21 NORMAN [shrugs]. None of my business.

Pause.

Not bothered about dances myself . . . dancing, I can take it, I can leave it . . . I'm easy.

He turns round to see if she is listening. She looks straight at him.

2 ENID. Every time he says, the fellar, every time he says 'Take Your Partners' I know . . . I know nobody's going to take me for a partner.

Pause.

3 NORMAN. Yes.

Pause.

Yes, I can see this creates . . . special problems for a girl . . . [*uncertain*].

4 ENID [*blank*]. You what?

5 NORMAN. Well, you know. . . . A man can ask a girl for a dance, but a girl, well, if nobody asks her . . . [*tails off uncertainly*].

6 ENID [*sarcastic*]. Brilliant, you, aren't you?

7 NORMAN. I'm sorry, I . . .

8 ENID [*sharp*]. Brilliant.

9 NORMAN. I didn't mean it like that, I didn't mean . . .

10 ENID. It doesn't matter, I don't care . . . I've told you now.

11 NORMAN. What about all the Test Pilots?

12 ENID. That's Jean. You can see them, gathering round ready. Course, there's only one of them can get there first, then they, like . . . look at me . . . and . . . [*tails off*]

Pause.

13 ENID. 'I don't like yours,' I've heard them saying that. 'I don't like yours. . . .'

14 NORMAN. The Northern Area Feather?

15 ENID. Bantam.

16 NORMAN. Bantamweight?

1 ENID. Jean.

2 NORMAN. And the poets. . . .

3 ENID. Jean.

      Pause.

4 NORMAN. Oh. So you came out here.

5 ENID. You get fed up. She went off with this lad. I usually
      find somewhere. [*indicates the pier*] You know.

6 NORMAN. It's being by yourself, that's the trouble. [*seeing her
      expression*] For me, I mean . . .

7 ENID. That's the trouble. Daft, isn't it? [*directly to* NORMAN] It's
      daft, isn't it?

8 NORMAN. What?

9 ENID. Everything. Everything's daft.

10 NORMAN. Model railways?

11 ENID. Test pilots.

12 NORMAN. Junior partnerships?

13 ENID. Broken legs, puffy noses, it's all daft.

14 NORMAN. I suppose it is.

      NORMAN *looks through telescope.*

15 ENID. It's still wet.

      Pause.

16 NORMAN [*trying to help*]. I know what you mean though. When
      I used to go dancing with the lads . . .

17 ENID. You had these three friends.

18 NORMAN. We had some good times—at least, they did.

19 ENID. What about you?

20 NORMAN. It's funny, saying this, daft I suppose, but I was
      always scared.

21 ENID. Scared?

22 NORMAN. Scared of asking anyone for a dance.

23 ENID [*shocked*]. What for?

1 NORMAN [*blandly*]. In case they said no.

2 ENID [*angry*]. You great idiot!

3 NORMAN [*shaken*]. I beg your pardon?

She follows him angrily around the pier as he tries to avoid her.

4 ENID. You're a twerp! What are you?

5 NORMAN [*bewildered*]. I'm sorry.

6 ENID. You're a twerp! What are you?

7 NORMAN. A twerp?

8 ENID. You know what you are? You're a twerp.

9 NORMAN. I said I was sorry.

10 ENID. So you should be.

11 NORMAN. I am.

By now he is cornered at the end of the pier near to the telescope.

12 ENID. The trouble with you is you're scared they'll say No.

13 NORMAN. That's what I said.

14 ENID. I know, I've got ears, haven't I? I never said you didn't.

15 NORMAN. I never said you did.

16 ENID. Shut up! You're mixing me up. I'll tell you why you're scared. Twerp.

17 NORMAN. I'm scared they'll say No.

18 ENID. You're scared because you're only thinking about yourself, number one. Poor little you, scared they'll say No. I know you. You stand at the side of the dance floor, smoking your pipe, trying to look all superior. I've seen dozens of twerps like you.

NORMAN *puts his pipe back in his pocket.*

But you never think about me, sitting at the other side of the floor, waiting to be asked . . . you're scared . . . scared other people might not love you as much as your Mother does. . . .

NORMAN *quickly moves to the telescope.*

1 ENID. Stop looking through that stupid thing!

2 NORMAN [*angry*]. It's a free country!

3 ENID. You haven't put a penny in!

4 NORMAN. That's my business.

5 ENID. You can't see anything if you don't put a penny in.

6 NORMAN. If I want to look at the sea. I'll look at it, even if I
   can't see it.

7 ENID. You should walk towards it and forget to stop!

8 NORMAN [*protesting*]. It's wet.

9 ENID [*shouting*]. I know it's bloody wet!

10 NORMAN [*losing control*]. We all know that! [*has another quick
   look*] It's saturated. . . .

11 ENID. Well what you arguing about then?

12 NORMAN. I'm not arguing.

   Pause.

   [*sadly*] Yes I am.

   ENID *sits on the bench, crying a mixture of anger, frustration and
   self-pity.* NORMAN *stands mournfully beside the telescope, wishing
   he could go home. There is a long pause during which the music of the
   last waltz is heard.*

13 ENID. Have to be getting back.

14 NORMAN. Good.

15 ENID. Last waltz.

   NORMAN *turns from his telescope and looks at* ENID *who is still
   dabbing her eyes, lightly. Very slowly he walks across to her and
   stands in front of her.*

16 NORMAN [*quietly*]. May I have this dance, please?

   Pause. ENID *stands up.*

17 ENID [*triumphant*]. No, you flaming well can't!

NORMAN *shrugs, takes postcards from his pocket, selects the appropriate card, puts the others in his pocket and walks slowly off along the pier.* ENID *watches him. She stands up.*

Yes.

2 NORMAN [*turning*]. Yes?

NORMAN *walks slowly back.*

3 NORMAN. Yes?

ENID *nods. They dance, uncertainly, not particularly well. Their conversation becomes animated, dance-hall-ish.*
They stumble slightly and stop dancing.

I'm sorry.

4 ENID. My fault.

5 NORMAN. No, my fault.

6 ENID. Wasn't anybody's fault.

They continue dancing.

7 NORMAN. I *am* sorry.

8 ENID. What for?

9 NORMAN. I think I made you . . . well, talking like that, making you. . . .

10 ENID [*flat*]. Making me cry.

11 NORMAN [*awkward*]. You're right, what you say, about smoking my pipe and . . .

12 ENID. Wasn't anybody's fault. [*casual*] I like dancing, it's . . .

Pause.

[*realizing*] Anyhow, you did ask me. . . .

13 NORMAN. Yes. I did ask you.

She stops dancing.

14 ENID. It's no good, you realize that, don't you?

15 NORMAN. I beg your pardon?

1 ENID. I mean, when I'm twenty-seven you'll be thirty-eight . . . [*pretending to be shocked*].

2 NORMAN [*catching on slowly*]. Oh, yes . . . yes, couldn't possibly work out.

   They continue dancing.

3 ENID. Couldn't possibly.

4 NORMAN. When I'm thirty-eight I'll be a . . . a boss.

5 ENID. You what?

6 NORMAN [*mock casual*]. I'm thinking of setting up on my own . . . just in the front room, at first. . . .

7 ENID. Our Terry, he reckons it's a good time for setting up on your own.

8 NORMAN. It's all tied up with the . . . [*confidential*] impending closure of the railways.

9 ENID [*cautious*]. You're not properly chartered. . . .

10 NORMAN. Neither's Cassius Clay and look at him . . . in lights, *and* Sandringham Lodge.

11 ENID [*anxious*]. Will your leg stand up to it, on cold days, like?

12 NORMAN. I'll think of something, don't worry. . . .

13 ENID. At least you haven't got a puffy nose, that's one thing. . . .

14 NORMAN. I like your nose.

15 ENID. You're wasting your time. When I'm thirty-nine, you'll be fifty. . . .

16 NORMAN [*shocked*]. I'm wasting my time.

17 ENID. You've got to be realistic.

18 NORMAN. Wouldn't be fair on the children.

19 ENID. Well, it's just for their sake, isn't it?

20 NORMAN. Of course, when I'm fifty I'll have a chain of front rooms, all over . . . all over the Northern Area.

21 ENID. The Northern Area?

22 NORMAN. Where the bantamweights come from. . . .

1 ENID. What you talking about? What's the matter with England?

2 NORMAN. [*The prospect increases.*] England, The British Isles. . . .

3 ENID. British Isles, Europe, the World . . . the Universe . . .

4 NORMAN. Watch this space! Millions of front rooms. . . .

5 ENID. All yours.

6 NORMAN [*quietly*]. Ours.

ENID stops dancing. NORMAN looks at her, very worried.

7 ENID [*very serious*]. When I'm a hundred and three. . . .

8 NORMAN. When you're nineteen, that's the important one.

Pause.

9 ENID. It isn't . . . like . . . isn't not fair on anybody then?

10 NORMAN [*sorting out grammar*]. It's fair . . . on everybody.

They kiss. They stop dancing and he starts conducted tour of the pier.

I'll be able to look after you, don't worry.

11 ENID. Look after me?

12 NORMAN. In the manner to which you've been accustomed.

13 ENID. I come from a rich family. You know . . . six wage packets coming in.

14 NORMAN [*casual*]. Consolidated Front Rooms had a record year.

15 ENID. With them shutting the railways?

16 NORMAN. Just opened a front room on the Riviera as a matter of fact.

17 ENID. The South of France.

Pause. She looks at sea.

Is that it?

18 NORMAN. Yes, that's it.

19 ENID. Is it really blue?

20 NORMAN. It's the sun shining on it.

1 ENID. It's the lights shining on it. It's best to go south in the winter.

2 NORMAN. Very dark it gets in the winter.

3 ENID. Well, you've got your leg to think about. . . .

4 NORMAN. I thought we'd have the swimming pool over there . . . [*points vaguely*].

5 ENID [*flatly*]. I can't swim.

6 NORMAN. For the children. I'll buy you a yacht. [*sniffs*] Can you smell the dahlias?

7 ENID. I'm always telling you, they're chrysanths—but you never listen.

8 NORMAN. It's my nose. It's puffy.

They laugh.

D'you really like it?

9 ENID. It's a lovely approach, bit like Sandringham . . .

10 NORMAN. You should have seen it last month.

11 ENID. I can hear the sea.

12 NORMAN. And concealed lighting, chap who designed it, he's very well chartered.

They sit down.

13 ENID. Is this the front room?

14 NORMAN. Do you like it?

15 ENID. It's better since we put the railway in the nursery.

16 NORMAN. It wasn't fair on the children.

17 ENID. Listen to the sea.

18 NORMAN. Can you see the lights?

19 ENID. I can hear the sea. It's like music.

20 NORMAN. Look.

21 ENID. Music in the sea.

22 NORMAN. Look.

23 ENID. Music . . . listen.

1 NORMAN. Used to be so grim in the winter.

2 ENID. Used to be dark in the winter.

3 NORMAN. You need the break from . . .

4 ENID. Being frightened.

    They kiss.

5 NORMAN [*listening to band playing National Anthem*]. I think they've
    stopped. . . .

6 ENID [*not too bothered*]. I said I'd meet Jean.

7 NORMAN. Thank you for the dance.

    NORMAN *stands up.*

8 ENID. I like dancing, it's . . .

9 NORMAN [*gently*]. I know.

10 ENID [*smiles*]. I can hear the sea.

    NORMAN *looks through telescope.*

11 NORMAN. Still there, still the same. *Almost* the same.

12 ENID. Wet.

    She looks at her watch.

13 NORMAN. Jean'll be waiting.

14 ENID. You've missed the post now. She can wait.

15 NORMAN. Give me your address, I'll send you one.

    Looks at his postcards.

    You won't want any of these.

    He throws them away.

16 ENID. Send me one with the lights on . . .

17 NORMAN. Will you be coming here again?

18 ENID. You need the break, don't you?

    The lights go out.

19 NORMAN. They've gone out.

1   ENID. Hasn't it gone dark?

     Pause.

2   NORMAN. No.

     Pause.

3   ENID. No.

     NORMAN *is beside the telescope,* ENID *near the bench—as they were when the illuminations were switched on.*

     The lights fade slowly to black.

Last Day in Dreamland

by Willis Hall

The scene is a dingy amusement arcade in a small northern seaside town.

CHARACTERS

FRANK COPPIN, manager

GEORGE FENTRILL

JACK MASON

TICH CURTIS

HARRY LOMAX

SAILOR BEESON

SANDERS

MIKE

ERNIE

PENELOPE

CUSTOMERS (non-speaking)

ACTING NOTE

✳ ✳ ✳
Last Day in Dreamland

It is nine a.m. and the arcade is not yet open. The room is in partial darkness, though a shaft of daylight streams through the plate glass doors at the entrance. We can see, high up on the walls, an odd assortment of grimy plaster gnomes, half-hidden in shadow and peering out from behind equally grimy plaster trees and shrubs. Through the glass doors we can see a deserted promenade. A man approaches, taking a bunch of keys from his pocket. He opens the front door and enters the arcade. He is FRANK COPPIN, *manager and mechanic in the arcade, a small thickset figure about fifty-two years of age.* COPPIN *walks down the length of the arcade and goes out through a door at the right-hand rear of the room and into the workshop. A moment later the lights are switched on in the arcade and we can now see the whole of the interior. The layout of the arcade looking in from the entrance is as follows:*

On the left is a darts stall and above this a 'marble alley'; on the right is a rifle range above which is the workshop. Across the rear of the arcade is a row of six or seven pin-tables. In the top left-hand corner of the arcade is a door leading to the toilets and a small cubicle which serves as the owner's office. The floor space in the centre is taken up with slot machines and pin-tables of all kinds. Above the stalls, in an inaccessible position, hang a variety of impressive prizes—huge teddy bears, tea services, etc.—these are never won and remain in the same position year after year. The smaller worthless prizes, mostly plaster figures: black cats, brown owls, etc., are on lower shelves. The final light to be switched on is a glaring neon sign hanging from the ceiling.

COPPIN *enters the arcade from the workshop. He is struggling into a knee-length denim overall, the breast pocket of which is stuffed with screwdrivers, spanners, etc. As* COPPIN *walks to the centre of the arcade* GEORGE FENTRILL *and* JACK MASON *enter through the main doors.* FENTRILL, *aged about twenty-eight, is the darts stall attendant. He is wearing a sports coat and flannels and carries a raincoat over his arm.* MASON, *about forty years old, tall and lean, is the rifle range attendant. He wears a drab serge suit and is also wearing a cheap raincoat and shapeless trilby.* FENTRILL *and* MASON *approach* COPPIN.

1   FENTRILL. Morning!

2   COPPIN. Morning, lads.

1   MASON. Morning, Frank. What's it going to be like, then?

2   COPPIN. Sunshine—we hope. Get a paper, did you?

> FENTRILL *tosses a morning paper to* COPPIN. FENTRILL *and* MASON *move off and go into the workshop.* COPPIN *glances at the sports page as* TICH CURTIS *enters through the main door.* CURTIS, *about fifty years old, is small and wiry, balding, neatly dressed though his clothes have seen a great deal of wear. He approaches* COPPIN.

3   CURTIS. Looks like being a good one, Frank.

> COPPIN *glances up from the paper.*

4   COPPIN. Morning, Tich.

> COPPIN *returns to his study of the paper but* CURTIS *refuses to take the hint.*

5   CURTIS. You heard anything, Frank?

6   COPPIN. What about?

7   CURTIS. I was wondering if the Governor had mentioned yet —when we were finishing this season, like.

8   COPPIN. Give over.

9   CURTIS. What's up?

> *During the following dialogue* FENTRILL *and* MASON *enter the arcade from the workshop. They have discarded their jackets and are now wearing hip-length denim coats—regulation uniform for all the staff with the exception of* COPPIN. FENTRILL *and* MASON *carry wash-leathers. The early morning duty of cleaning up the arcade has been brought to a fine art and is executed swiftly—*MASON *wipes the glass fronts and tops of the machines with a wet leather and* FENTRILL *follows up with a dry leather.* COPPIN *folds the paper carefully.*

10   COPPIN. Tich, you ought to make a record. You ought to put it on an L.P. You ought to be on the Hit Parade. Top Ten.

11   CURTIS. I was only wondering if the Guv had said anything, Frank.

12   COPPIN. Fourteen years you been wondering. Every year we get towards the end of the season—September, October

—every week you come up with the same question:
'You heard anything, Frank?' Does he ever tell me when
we're packing it in?

2 CURTIS. I just thought he might, that's all.

3 COPPIN. The jackpot question. Give him the money, Mabel.
Go on, you bald-headed old burk—get this place swept
up.

4 CURTIS. It was just that I was wondering.

CURTIS crosses towards workshop. MASON *is scrubbing energetically
at a glass-topped pin-table.*

5 MASON. Candy-floss. Rotten candy-floss. Kids with a fistful of
candy-floss should be barred from coming in.

6 FENTRILL. Ah—stop moaning.

7 MASON. You haven't got to shift the stuff off these machines
—it's murder. Kids hanging over the playing footballer
and slavering candy-floss and chewing gum. There
should be a bloke on the door. Permanent. Sailor should
be on the door—he should be stopping them from
coming in.

8 FENTRILL. Moan, moan, moan. Try giving it a rest, boy. Let
your tonsils have a holiday.

9 MASON. Who are you talking to?

10 FENTRILL. You. That's who. You.

11 MASON. If you want to do the leathering I'll wipe.

12 FENTRILL. Who's talking about leathering?

13 MASON. If you had to leather it off these machines you'd
moan. Why let them in sucking that muck? That's all
I'm saying.

14 FENTRILL. Wittle, wittle, wittle.

15 MASON. Dry up, George. That's all—just dry up.

MASON, *having removed the stains from the glass top, moves on to the
next machine as* FENTRILL *begins to wipe the leathered glass dry.*
HARRY LOMAX *enters through the main door. He is a young man—
about twenty years of age—and is the attendant on the row of*

pin-tables at the rear of the arcade—dressed in an open-necked shirt and jeans. His first greeting is addressed to no one in particular.

1 LOMAX. Morning all!

2 COPPIN. It's nearly ten past.

3 LOMAX. It never is!

LOMAX crosses to FENTRILL and MASON as CURTIS enters from workshop. CURTIS is now wearing his regulation jacket and carries a large sweeping brush. He begins to sweep down one side of the arcade starting from the rear. LOMAX examines the machine that FENTRILL is polishing with the wash-leather.

Very good. Smashing. You've made a lovely job of that, George.

4 FENTRILL. Rot off.

5 LOMAX. Got a penny?

6 FENTRILL. What's up, like? Do you want to go in the Ladies?

7 LOMAX. I want to weigh myself.

8 FENTRILL. I'll tell you that for nothing. Five stone six.

9 LOMAX. Come on, come on—less of the patter. Give us a coin.

FENTRILL digs in his pockets.

10 FENTRILL. What's it for?

11 LOMAX. I'm out of smokes. I want to win myself a snout.

FENTRILL hands him a penny. LOMAX crosses to play a machine, FENTRILL calls after him.

12 FENTRILL. Gambling now. What's your mother going to say to that? I don't know where you'll end up, I'm sure.

LOMAX plays the machine and loses. He bangs the glass front with the palm of his hand.

13 COPPIN. Break it, lad. I should.

14 LOMAX. It's a fiddle. It's a rotten carve up! This swindle never pays out.

15 COPPIN [*not unkindly*]. Come on, Harry, it's ten past nine all but.

1 LOMAX. You want to get this fiddle seen to, that's all.

2 FENTRILL. No good if you do win. Them fags have been in there since April—he hasn't filled it up since then. I got one out myself yesterday and smoked it. I was sick twice.

3 COPPIN. When you've quite finished, all of you—we might get this place cleared up for dinner time.

4 LOMAX. All right—I'm coming.

LOMAX crosses towards workshop passing CURTIS on the way.

5 CURTIS. You want a fag, do you, Harry!

6 LOMAX. S'alright, Tich—got some in my other jacket.

LOMAX goes into workshop. CURTIS lengthens his strokes as he sweeps the arcade and breaks loudly into song.

7 CURTIS. Come into the garden, Maud, for the black bat night has flown.

8 FENTRILL. You can wrap that up before you start.

9 CURTIS. Come into the garden, Maud, I am here at the gate alone.

10 FENTRILL. You will be if you carry on like that much longer.

11 MASON. He's a good turn but he's on too long.

12 FENTRILL. Who's asking you!

13 MASON. Shut up.

LOMAX enters from workshop with sweeping brush and sweeps down the arcade on the opposite side to CURTIS. COPPIN crosses to FENTRILL and returns newspaper.

14 COPPIN. Thanks.

15 FENTRILL. Ta, Frank.

16 COPPIN. How's the missis, then?

17 FENTRILL. All right. Smashing. She went in this morning.

18 COPPIN. A bit early, isn't it?

19 FENTRILL. 'Bout a week. One minute she's washing up—next

thing I know I'm getting her clobber together. Neighbour's going to ring up if anything happens.

2 COPPIN. I see.

3 FENTRILL. Be all right that? Use the phone?

4 COPPIN. Course. Why not?

> MASON *has now finished his duties with the wash-leather. During the following dialogue he returns the leather to the workshop and takes up his position by the rifle range.*

5 FENTRILL. Be glad when it's all over, any road.

6 COPPIN. Yeh. What do you want?

7 FENTRILL. We're not bothered—least I'm not. She's after a little lass. Could have done with having it the beginning of the season—you know, expense—we could have managed better then.

> FENTRILL *moves across to wipe dry the last machine.* COPPIN *follows* FENTRILL *across to the machine.*

8 COPPIN. These things will happen.

> FENTRILL *finishes his task.*

9 FENTRILL. That's how it goes. . . . That's about the lot. I don't suppose you've heard anything? When he is finishing?

10 COPPIN. Could be any time. Today happen. Might stretch another week out of it. I don't know. The weather's picked up but the town's dead. This week's been rotten —losing money. It's hopeless.

11 FENTRILL. Yeh.

12 COPPIN. So—you know what the boss is like. Same every year —he packs in when it suits him, when he feels like it. One morning he comes in—has a little trot as far as the door and a gander at the pitch. Turns round—always the same spiel. 'We've had it, lads. Finishing tonight. Best of luck. See you next season.' So—nine p.m. you cop your wages and a bit of bonus and an early night. Shake hands all round and another year's gone.

LOMAX has hastily caught up with CURTIS by the entrance. They sweep the dust on to a shovel, return the brushes to the workshop and take up their position on their respective stalls during the following dialogue.

1 FENTRILL. I reckon I'm going to get out of this lark.

2 COPPIN. They all say the same the end of the season.

3 FENTRILL. This is straight up, Frank. Next year I'll be out of it. Grafting steady.

4 COPPIN. You said that last year.

5 FENTRILL. Last year was different.

6 COPPIN. And the year before.

7 FENTRILL. I left it too late last year. I should have scarpered as soon as the season ended.

8 COPPIN. You've been saying it every year.

9 FENTRILL. This year I worked it out. How you slip up, I mean. See—as soon as you get your cards you should hop it. Blow. No good hanging about the town, or else you— sort of—let things slide.

10 COPPIN. You and a thousand others.

11 FENTRILL. With the nipper coming it'll have to be different. You can't keep a family on dole and N.A.

12 COPPIN. There's plenty tries. Less than a fortnight now and there'll be hundreds queueing up outside the Labour twice a week.

13 FENTRILL. Not me this year, you can count on that. Go to a place like Birmingham or Leeds or Coventry or any-where like that—inland—there must be jobs going. You know, regular jobs. All the year round. Well, that's what I'm reckoning on.

14 COPPIN. I'll believe it when I see it.

15 FENTRILL. San fairy ann to this caper. It's my last season, boy.

FENTRILL crosses to the darts stall and, as he passes the 'marble alley', he steals a cigarette which CURTIS has just lit and placed on his counter while he dusts the prizes. CURTIS sings happily.

1   CURTIS. Oh, God bless you and keep you, Mother Machree.

> CURTIS *turns to pick up his cigarette, notices it is missing and crosses immediately to the darts stall. He extends his hand.*

2   FENTRILL. What's up, Tich?

3   CURTIS. My fag.

> FENTRILL *examines the cigarette he is smoking.*

4   FENTRILL. Is it yours? I must have picked it up by mistake. However did I come to do that?

> FENTRILL *returns the cigarette.*

5   CURTIS. You can't catch me like that, George. I get up too early of a morning.

> CURTIS *returns to his stall as* FENTRILL *calls after him.*

6   FENTRILL. You're all there, Tich. You've got it up here, boy.

> *As he speaks, and while* CURTIS *has his back to him,* FENTRILL *leans across and steals two small prizes from* CURTIS'S *stall and places them among his own.* CURTIS *climbs on to his stall to dust the 'unwinnable' prizes above. He flicks the dust from a giant teddy bear and again bursts into song.*

7   CURTIS. Poems are made by fools like me, but only God can make a tree.

> FENTRILL *leans round the corner of the darts stall.*

8   FENTRILL. Why don't you give it a rest?

9   CURTIS. You don't appreciate good music, that's all.

10   FENTRILL. You won't appreciate having that furry animal rammed down your throat.

> CURTIS *accepts the warning philosophically and hums the rest of the tune to himself.* COPPIN *crosses to* FENTRILL.

11   COPPIN. Seen anything of Sailor yet, George?

12   FENTRILL. Hasn't he turned in?

13   COPPIN. Not to my knowledge.

1   FENTRILL. You know Sailor. He'll roll up—when he's ready. He doesn't care.

2   COPPIN. He'll manage this trick once too often. Come rolling in one morning when the boss is here—land right in it.

3   FENTRILL. Good old Sailor.

4   COPPIN. He'll slip up—one of these days. How are you off for swag, then?

     FENTRILL *glances round and swiftly surmises the number of prizes on his shelves.*

5   FENTRILL. All right. Given nothing away this week. Taken nothing either. We've had it for this year.

     COPPIN *moves away.*

6   COPPIN. Just about.

     MASON *crosses to the darts stall, picks up a set of darts and throws them into the board.* FENTRILL *retrieves the darts and places them on the counter.*

7   MASON. S'ave a look at your paper, George.

     FENTRILL *takes the folded newspaper from his pocket and hands it to* MASON.

8   FENTRILL. You can buy them, you know. In shops. Two-pence ha'penny.

     MASON *turns to the sports page.*

9   MASON. Why should I spend good money when I can borrow yours?

10   FENTRILL. What have you got today, then?

11   MASON. Three little beauties, boy, that's all. Three little gems. A pile of certs.

12   FENTRILL. Tell me the old, old story.

13   MASON. They're laid on, George. Past the post already these three. You want to come in with me? One thirty—two o'clock and two-thirty—all at Donnie. Slip me half a bar and we'll make it a quid treble. All outsiders.

1 FENTRILL. What! And me a family man almost. I should nobbit.

LOMAX *crosses to join them.*

2 LOMAX. Sorted them out, have you, Jack?

3 FENTRILL. You know his horses. Jack's selected. They'll still be running tomorrow.

4 MASON. You wait till they romp home, son, and I'm in the money. You want to come in for ten bob, Harry?

5 LOMAX. On a Friday? I'm boracic.* Subbed his nibs for a nicker already.

LOMAX *picks up three darts from the counter and tosses them into the dartboard.* FENTRILL *retrieves them and returns them to the counter.*

6 FENTRILL. Give it a rest. I ought to start charging you blokes for this caper.

MASON *glances towards the entrance.*

7 MASON. Here he is! The one and only! Where have you been to, shipmate of mine?

FENTRILL *and* LOMAX *turn towards entrance as* SAILOR BEESON *enters and crosses towards the darts stall.* BEESON *is in his late sixties but looks much older—a shabby, balding man in a roll neck seaman's navy blue jersey. He is already wearing the 'regulation' jacket.*

8 FENTRILL. Hello then! It's Dirty Dan the Dustbin Man who comes but once a year.

9 BEESON. Morning, lads.

10 MASON. Good morning, he says, and it's afternoon.

11 FENTRILL. What have you been on, like, you dirty old devil? Night on the tiles?

12 BEESON. Have you finished the cleaning up?

13 MASON. What's it look like? You don't half work it. Where've you been then?

* Cockney rhyming slang; short for 'boracic lint' = skint or stony broke.

128

BEESON *takes a battered watch from his breast pocket. He examines it, shakes it, and holds it to his ear.*

1 BEESON. It has. It's stopped again.

2 FENTRILL. It's like you, you mouldy old louse-pot. It wants slinging. It's not a dickory-dock you want, admiral, it's a missis—somebody that can kick you out of bed in a morning.

3 MASON. He'd never get up at all then.

COPPIN *crosses to join them.*

4 COPPIN. What's your excuse this morning, Sailor?

BEESON *pats his breast pocket.*

5 BEESON. My watch again. I must have forgot to wind it up.

6 COPPIN. Never lets you down when it's going home time. You want to hang on to that one. It must be a good one.

7 BEESON. I'm thinking of buying a new one.

8 COPPIN. Well, while you're turning the idea over in your mind, you can be giving the firm a hand. You can fetch a jug of tea from round the johnny-horner.

9 BEESON. Backards and forrards. Backards and forrards. We ought to have a lad for errands.

10 FENTRILL. Why should we when we've got you? The oldest young man on the prom. How's that for a fiddle? We rig up a bit of canvas round him and knock the mugs a bob apiece to have a skeg.

11 LOMAX. Who's going to pay to see him?

12 FENTRILL. Trippers, sonny. They pay to see anything. Jack'll tell you. A smashing fiddle one year. Bob a time. The Fall of China. Nip in and a geezer drops half a dozen cups on the floor. That's it. 'Move along at the front, please, and let them at the back come in.'

13 LOMAX. Go on!

14 FENTRILL. It's straight up, lad. Them were the good old days. Remember the Man Eating Cod, Jack? Charge you a

tanner to see a bloke sitting down with a fish and four pennorth.

2 MASON. Them were the days.

3 FENTRILL. Just after the war when the town was crammed with loaded Yanks.

4 MASON. It'll never be the same again.

5 FENTRILL. Wait and see. I've got the finest little fiddle fixed up for next season.

6 LOMAX. What's that?

7 FENTRILL. Me and Jack. This is the boy—Melody Mason, the perpetual pianist. Plays for a week without stopping. Genuine. Money refunded to dissatisfied customers. How about that, eh, Tosh?

8 MASON. I'll put my name down for piano lessons.

9 FENTRILL. What? And give them music as well? Just thump it, that's all. You could do it with your feet.... Hey! That's not a bad idea! Twinkletoes Mason—born with his brains in his heels. We could carve up a fortune.

10 COPPIN. If things don't pick up soon we look like losing one. Come on, Sailor, what about that tea?

11 BEESON. Just going. [*He crosses to entrance of the arcade, glances along the deserted promenade and turns to call back into the arcade.*] Nobody about yet. Front's dead. He'll about close today, I reckon.

12 FENTRILL. That's right. Cheer us all up.

13 BEESON. Just saying what it looks like. [*exit along the front*]

14 COPPIN. Come on, Harry, you can give me a hand. I'll have the front off that machine while it's quiet.

15 LOMAX. Right.

COPPIN *and* LOMAX *move up to the end of the arcade.*

16 MASON. He's right, you know. Today could see the end of it.

FENTRILL *takes out a packet of cigarettes, gives one to* MASON, *takes out a box of matches and lights his own and* MASON'S *cigarette.*

MASON, meanwhile, has thrown three darts into a board. FENTRILL
retrieves darts.

1 FENTRILL. Give it a rest.
2 MASON. Do you think we will?
3 FENTRILL. What's that?
4 MASON. Finish today?
5 FENTRILL. How should I know?
6 MASON. Come on, I'll give you a game. Chase you round the
   board—on the doubles.
7 FENTRILL. No, thanks.
8 MASON. Tanner stakes? Three hundred and one up?
9 FENTRILL. Forget the darts, will you!
10 MASON. Just an idea. Pass the time on.
11 FENTRILL. You know what I want, right now? I'll tell you
   what we could do with, shall I? Trippers.
12 MASON. Some hopes.
13 FENTRILL. Just one works outing, boy. That's all—just one. A
   puffer train stuffed with mugs and trippers. Enough to
   see us over the weekend. Couple of hundred hard-case
   teds in cardboard bobbies' helmets and crêpe creepers.
   Three or four score of giggling skirts on a day off from a
   rag factory. Little lasses with high hopes of matrimony,
   a stick of rock in one hand, giant humbug in the other
   and their handbags stuffed with 'True Romances' and 'I
   Was a Teenage Sex Maniac'.
14 MASON. It's the wrong end of the season.
15 FENTRILL. Just one train-load, that's all I'm asking. Bit of
   encouragement for the Governor and we could drag
   another week out of it.
16 MASON. Today's the day, George. We've had it. Let's face it.

   CURTIS, *who has now climbed down from the counter and is indus-*
   triously cleaning the row of small prizes, breaks into song.

17 CURTIS. But for all that I found there, I might as well be—
   Where the mountains of Mourne sweep down to the
   sea.

1 FENTRILL. Shut up. [*to* MASON] Ah, come on—I'll give you that game.

2 MASON. Round the board?

3 FENTRILL. On the doubles.

4 MASON. Tanner stakes?

5 FENTRILL [*nods*]. You kick off.

FENTRILL and MASON begin their game of darts. COPPIN and LOMAX are repairing a pin-table. The glass top of the machine has been removed and COPPIN is making some slight adjustment to the playing board with a screwdriver.

6 COPPIN. Ready for the big push then?

7 LOMAX. Just about.

8 COPPIN. Any plans, have you?

9 LOMAX. Just move on, that's all. Drift.

10 COPPIN. One season of this lark enough for you, is it?

11 LOMAX. You can say that again. I mean, it's been all right, you know, Frank. Passed the summer on and that. I don't know. . . . I wouldn't fancy another season at it.

12 COPPIN. No. . . . I think that's about got it.

COPPIN has completed his adjustment of the machine. With the help of LOMAX he slides the glass back into position.

Thanks.

COPPIN and LOMAX turn and lean their backs against the machines, surveying the arcade. LOMAX takes out a packet of cigarettes, offers one to COPPIN who refuses, and lights one himself.

13 LOMAX. Boy, if this place was ever dead.

14 COPPIN. It's that time of year. After July and August it's all over. Any day now. When the shutters do go up—you bunk, son. Get your skates on—no messing.

15 LOMAX. For sure.

16 COPPIN. Inland. Away from the tripper trade.

17 LOMAX. First train out.

1 COPPIN. What kind of a job are you looking for?

LOMAX *shrugs his shoulders.*

2 LOMAX. I'm easy.

3 COPPIN. Nothing in mind?

4 LOMAX. Nothing special. Well . . .

5 COPPIN. Yeh?

6 LOMAX. You know what I'd like, Frank? Straight up. What would just about suit my number.

7 COPPIN. What's that?

8 LOMAX. Driving. You know—lorries and that. Up the Great North. Right up the A1, man. Sitting up there in my own cab—eight wheeler—grabbing the wheel. No bosses. Just charging up the Great North.

9 COPPIN. Done any driving ever, have you?

10 LOMAX. A bit. Some in the army.

11 COPPIN. If that's what you want it sounds a good idea.

12 LOMAX. I mean—you know—so one day I might have my own truck even. Working for myself.

13 COPPIN. Why not?

14 LOMAX. Yeh, why not? . . . I suppose. . . . But who'd set me on?

15 COPPIN. You can only try.

16 LOMAX. I mean, there's stacks of drivers out of work already —so what chance would I have?

17 COPPIN. Inland you could try.

18 LOMAX. Who'd want to give me a job?

19 COPPIN. No harm in asking.

20 LOMAX. What's the use?

21 COPPIN. You've got to try, son! So all right, if it gets you nowhere, what've you got to lose?

22 LOMAX. There's that about it.

23 COPPIN. When I was your age, Harry, you know what I had in mind?

1 LOMAX. What's that?

2 COPPIN. One day I was going to have my own shop. Mending
wirelesses—they were all the go then. A little shop,
somewhere, house to go with it perhaps. Happen a lad
set on to give me a hand. So that was going to be me:
radio mechanic, electrician—nice bit of retail as well,
posh front and the window decked out with swag. I had
it all worked out.

3 LOMAX. So what happened?

4 COPPIN. Nothing. That's all—nothing. For years I talked
about having that shop—the summers I've spent in here
dreaming about that joint don't bear thinking about. So
one day, before you know where you are, you're fifty-
two and all you've got is a screwdriver, a fistful of loose
change and six months' work a year.

5 LOMAX. You haven't done too bad.

6 COPPIN. I'm not complaining. I'm just telling you. Get out
of it, son. When the season folds, you scarper.

7 LOMAX. I'm not staying.

8 COPPIN. Nobody ever is. Neither was George or Tich but they
turn up every year—next summer they'll be back.

BENSON *enters through main entrance and crosses arcade, approach-*
ing COPPIN *and* LOMAX. *He is carrying two jugs of tea.*

9 BEESON. Tea up. The tide's in.

10 COPPIN. Stick mine in the workshop, Sailor. I'll be in.

BEESON *goes into workshop.*

11 LOMAX. One season's enough for this boy.

12 COPPIN. So just you keep it that way. It's a long winter.

COPPIN *goes into the workshop as* BEESON *comes out carrying a*
single jug of tea. LOMAX *crosses to* BEESON.

13 LOMAX. Here, cop me that, Sailor. I'll see to it.

BEESON *hands the jug to* LOMAX.

1 BEESON. That's for Jack and George and Tich and you. Mine's in the back.

2 LOMAX. Right.

BEESON *goes into the workshop as* LOMAX *crosses arcade towards the darts stall. As* LOMAX *approaches,* FENTRILL *and* MASON *finish off their game of darts.* MASON *crosses to rifle range and returns with a small mug.* FENTRILL *takes two small mugs from beneath counter for* LOMAX *and himself.* LOMAX *calls out to* CURTIS *as he passes the marble alley.*

Tea up, Tich!

3 CURTIS. O.K., Harry!

LOMAX *places the jug of tea on the counter of the darts stall.*

4 FENTRILL. Here's the lad I've been waiting to see all morning. Good old Harry. I've been gagging for this.

MASON *places his mug on the counter.*

5 MASON. Get it sorted out, then, and less of the patter.

6 FENTRILL. Who are you talking to?

7 MASON. I'm telling you—pour the tea!

FENTRILL *raises the jug menacingly.*

8 FENTRILL. You want it pouring, you can have it pouring. Right down your mush.

CURTIS *approaches with his mug which he places on the counter.*

9 CURTIS. Here you are, George.

10 FENTRILL. What do you want then, Caruso?

11 CURTIS. My tea.

12 FENTRILL. Out of this jug? Four of us! I should cocoa.

13 MASON. Will you dish it out!

14 FENTRILL. Four of us out of this jug and there's Nosher Coppin and Popeye the Sailor stretched out in the back gobbing a jug of tea between them! What's my name? Doctor Barnardo?

1 CURTIS. Come on, George, it'll get cold.

2 MASON. Pour the rotten tea!

FENTRILL *pours the tea reluctantly.*

3 FENTRILL. One jug for four of us—it gets worse every morning.

They drink. FENTRILL *takes a short pull at his mug and slams it down on the counter.*

4 MASON. What's up now?

5 FENTRILL. No stinking sugar!

6 MASON. Get it down you and stop griping.

7 CURTIS. It's all right, George—it's wet and warm.

8 FENTRILL. It's like you then.

BEESON *enters from workshop carrying a mug of tea. He crosses towards the darts stall.*

What happened to the tea this morning?

9 BEESON. I fetched it. You've got it.

10 FENTRILL. Where's the rest?

11 BEESON. There isn't any rest. Only two jugs this morning, George.

12 FENTRILL. Don't give me that. You see yourself all right, you old twister—you greedy old swill-bin.

13 BEESON. It's hard carrying three. It spills over and burns your hand.

14 FENTRILL. You want burning, and all, you do. If I haven't had enough. If I don't get out of this set-up and start grafting away from the water. When this season folds I'm away with the mixer.

15 CURTIS. Do you think the Guv'll pack it in tonight, George?

16 FENTRILL. How should I know? Tonight! The way things are going we'll be out of work for dinner.

17 MASON. It's dead, boy. We've had it for this year—that's for certain.

1   LOMAX. You can say that again.

2   FENTRILL. We'll have the Governor walk in any minute. Look
at it! Just look at it! Not a soul! I haven't took a penny
—not a rotten coin since we opened. So what's happened to the mugs!

*FENTRILL glances around the empty arcade and then down towards
the entrance as the first* CUSTOMER *of the day enters—an inconse-
quential man in a raincoat and trilby.*

We've started. Come on . . . come on, you little beauty.

*The atmosphere changes instantly and the attendants are suddenly
businesslike.* MASON *crosses to the rifle range.* LOMAX *crosses to the
pin-tables at rear.* CURTIS *crosses to the marble alley and* BEESON
positions himself among the slot machines in the centre of the arcade.
FENTRILL *places all the mugs beneath the counter of the darts stall
and wipes the top of the counter with a duster. The* CUSTOMER,
*unaware of the activity his entarnce has caused, pauses to examine a
machine and then strolls down the arcade approaching the rifle range.*
MASON'S *approach to the customer is conversational.*

3   MASON. Try the guns, sir? All balanced and tested. Four shots
for sixpence. Score nineteen or over you take any prize
on the bottom shelf. Try the shooting, sir. How about
the rifles? Only nineteen and you get a prize. All guns
balanced and tested.

The CUSTOMER *pauses at the rifle range and walks along the rear of
the arcade, passing to examine a machine as* LOMAX *calls out.*

4   LOMAX. Change! Any change or copper required! Change—
any change! Get your change, then! Change or copper!
Score two hundred and fifty or over you get a prize!
Change any change!

The CUSTOMER *moves on, approaching the marble alley.* CURTIS
calls out to him in a mild, sad voice.

5   CURTIS. Here you are then, sir. Roll them down to win a
prize. You get five balls for sixpence and there are eight
winning numbers. Eight winning numbers, sir. If you

score five or thirty you take any prize on the stall. Any prize on the stall for sixpence only. Only sixpence and five and thirty take the pick of the stall.

The CUSTOMER *again moves on.* MASON, LOMAX, BEESON *and* CURTIS *watch him apprehensively. It has become imperative to them that the customer should spend some money—in fact, for the moment, their livelihood depends upon it—or so it would seem. Fate hangs upon* FENTRILL *who is the perfect 'joint-man'. He alternatively bullies, cajoles and entices the customer to play darts.*

2 FENTRILL. Hey. Hey, Jack. Just a minute. You. I mean you, mister. I'm talking to you!

The CUSTOMER *turns in surprise and then shakes his head.*

No, no, no, no. No, I don't want you to play darts. I want to show you something. Come here a tick.

The CUSTOMER *hesitates.*

Come on, my old flower. Have a look at this. Not for darts! I wouldn't ask you to play darts, my old son.

The CUSTOMER *crosses to the darts stall.* LOMAX, BEESON, MASON *and* CURTIS *are relieved.* FENTRILL *has triumphed.* FENTRILL *glances swiftly around the stall for something to maintain the* CUSTOMER'S *interest and then takes one of the mugs from beneath the counter.*

Look at that then. It's had tea in it. . . . No! Wait! Don't go away. I've not finished yet. I've got something to tell you, my old cock-sparrow. I'm going to do you a bit of good, my old lad. Because do you know what I'm going to do for you? You don't know, do you? Well let me finish. I'm going to tell you. You're my first customer today—so—listen—so—you see what it says up there? It says sixty-five or over. Right? Now keep this to yourself because I'm not supposed to do it.

FENTRILL *lowers his voice.*

I'm going to give you ten start. No kidding. You get fifty-five or over I'm going to give you a prize. I can't say fairer than that, can I? Well, come on, my old love, don't stand there weighing it up. Slip us your tanner! Let's be holding.

The CUSTOMER *pays* FENTRILL *and throws his first dart.*

2 LOMAX. Good old George.

3 MASON. Off we go again. That lad could squeeze it out of a stone.

4 CURTIS. If George can hang on to him and work up a pitch before the Guv gets in we'll be all right for another week.

5 BEESON. George has got him.

FENTRILL *has retrieved the darts from the board and replaces them on the counter.*

6 FENTRILL. Sixteen and ten is twenty-six and double top's sixty-six. Very good. That's a winner, my old lad. That's one win. Let's you in on the bottom shelf. Now then, my old china, you have another go and you win again, you move up there—second shelf—getting in among the big stuff. Let's be having your tanner then.

The CUSTOMER *hands* FENTRILL *another coin which he places in the box, with the first, at the rear of the stall. A* SECOND CUSTOMER— *a young man—enters the arcade and walks around examining the machines. A record player, controlled from the workshop and wired to loudspeakers around the arcade, begins to play a 'pop' tune. The other attendants shout ad-libs from their respective stalls.*

Here we are then! Here's another lucky winner! Who says the jolly old darts!

The CUSTOMER *takes up the darts as* BOB SANDERS, *the arcade proprietor, enters through main entrance.* SANDERS *is about forty-five years old, neatly dressed—a quiet businessman and not the usual flashy spiv-type character associated with amusement arcades.* SANDERS *walks down the arcade and approaches the darts stall as the* CUSTOMER *is about to throw his first dart.*

Morning, Guv!

1 SANDERS. Morning, George. [*He moves on, approaching marble alley.*]

2 CURTIS. Nice morning, Mr. Sanders.

3 SANDERS. We could do with it. Any good this morning?

4 CURTIS. Not yet. Bit too early. Might pick up towards dinner time, though—hard to tell.

COPPIN *enters from workshop and crosses to* SANDERS.

5 COPPIN. Morning!

6 SANDERS. Hello, Frank. [*He glances around the arcade.*] Bit thin?

7 COPPIN. Bit too thin for my liking—getting towards the end of it.

SANDERS *and* COPPIN *move away from the marble alley and approach the rear of the arcade.* CURTIS *goes into his spiel almost desperately.*

8 CURTIS. Here you are! Five balls for sixpence! Eight winning numbers and you score five or thirty you take any prize on show.

9 SANDERS. Anything much at all this morning?

10 COPPIN. This is the first sign of life we've had. I was talking to Fred Carter last night—runs the joint on the South Pier—he's not done a fiver since Monday.

11 SANDERS. He's not the only one.

12 COPPIN. So it's any day now?

13 SANDERS. Looks that way . . . I don't know. . . . Once a year you pack it in so once a year you pay off half a dozen blokes, so once a year you can't stand the sight of yourself.

14 COPPIN. It's not your fault. It's the living. It's the tripper trade. That's how it goes.

15 SANDERS. It's no consolation for the lads.

16 COPPIN. They know how it is. They come into the business. They don't blame you.

A telephone rings in SANDERS's *office.*

1 SANDERS. No. . . . Hang on a sec.

> SANDERS *goes into his office and picks up the phone.* CURTIS *is still going on with his spiel.*

2 CURTIS. Five balls for sixpence then! Roll 'em down! Eight winning numbers and five balls for sixpence.

3 COPPIN. Pack it in, Tich. Give it a rest. You're talking to yourself.

> SANDERS *enters from the office and moves down to the darts stall. The* CUSTOMER *has finished playing and is now deciding upon his prize.*

4 SANDERS. George—phone for you.

5 FENTRILL. Thanks, Guv. Be there in a sec.

> SANDERS *walks down to the entrance and stands looking out along the deserted sea-front.* FENTRILL *turns to the* CUSTOMER.

Made your mind up yet, my old flower-pot? Look— where were you? Second shelf? You're my first customer today so I'll tell you what I'm going to do—but don't let it get around. [FENTRILL *takes a small plastic butter dish from the shelf and places it on the counter.*]
How's that for you? Butter dish. Genuine plastic. Two wins. Take it—quick—before I change my mind. We're closed.

> FENTRILL *vaults over the counter and crosses to rear of arcade. During the following dialogue both customers leave the arcade and the record player stops. As* FENTRILL *passes the marble alley* COPPIN *calls after him.*

6 COPPIN. Get a shift on, George, she's waiting for you!

7 CURTIS. George's missis?

> FENTRILL *enters the office and closes the door.*

8 COPPIN. Sounds like it. He took her in last night. They reckon on it being some time today.

> MASON *crosses to the marble alley.*

1 MASON. Has it happened?

2 COPPIN. That's what we're waiting to find out.

LOMAX and BEESON cross to the marble alley.

3 BEESON. What's up, Frank.

4 COPPIN. I've just said. . . . Oh, never mind, you old nit. I'll send you a postcard.

5 MASON. It's George's missis. She's having a snapper.

6 BEESON. Go on! When's that

7 COPPIN. Pancake Tuesday—when do you think?

The group turn towards the office door as it opens and FENTRILL enters, closing the door carefully behind him. He walks slowly down the arcade, approaches the group at the marble alley, passes, and looks up.

8 FENTRILL. Hey! Seven pounds fifteen rotten ounces! It's a little lad! Seven bloody pounds fifteen ounces!

9 MASON. Good old dad!

10 CURTIS. How's the missis, George? Is the missis all right, George?

11 FENTRILL. Yeh! The pair of 'em!

COPPIN, MASON, CURTIS, LOMAX and BEESON crowd upon FENTRILL and ad-lib congratulations. SANDERS crosses down arcade from the entrance—he is unaware of the above dialogue. As he approaches the group their conversation dies away.

12 SANDERS. We've . . . we've about had it, lads. Might as well pack it in tonight. I'll pay you all to next Friday—not much point in carrying on. Anyhow, there'll be jobs for you next season—if you want them, that is. I thought we might have stretched it out another week or two. Not much sense. Only losing money.

SANDERS goes into the office. The group breaks up—the attendants return to their respective stalls. CURTIS is left alone at the marble alley. He stands on the 'playing side' of the stall and rolls five balls down the board disinterestedly, singing quietly to himself.

1 CURTIS. So I just took a hand at this digging for gold. But for all that I found there I might as well be—Where the mountains of Mourne sweep down to the sea.

The lights fade.

SCENE 2 FOUR HOURS LATER

It is two p.m. and MASON, FENTRILL *and* BEESON *are out at lunch.* LOMAX *has taken over the darts stall in* FENTRILL'S *absence,* CURTIS *is on the marble alley and* COPPIN *stands at the rear of the arcade. As the lights fade up we discover two youths,* ERNIE *and* MICK, *lounging against a machine in the centre of the arcade.* ERNIE *is playing the machine, which is of the 'five-ball-a-penny' variety.* MICK *is losing his temper.*

2 MICK. So all right. I don't mind. We'll hear your suggestion.

3 ERNIE. I don't know. I just don't want to go, that's all.

4 MICK. So you don't want to go. What do we do then? Stick in this lousy dump and blue a nicker?

ERNIE plays the first ball. He watches its progress round the board.

5 ERNIE. No. . . . I don't know. I don't mind. I just don't want to meet them bints—that's all.

6 MICK. Last night you were dead keen.

7 ERNIE. I can change my mind. You go if you want.

8 MICK. Sure. I can see me lumbered with two of them. What should I do with two bints?

9 ERNIE. You could lose one.

10 MICK. You're just being awkward now—just for the sake of being awkward.

ERNIE plays the second ball.

11 ERNIE. What's awkward got to do with it? If I don't want to see the skirt I don't want to see her—that's all.

12 MICK. Who asked me to cut in on the birds? Who asked me to break up the quickstep and line them up? For this afternoon? Eh?

1   ERNIE. They were right the other end of the dance floor. I hadn't seen them close up.

2   MICK. You wanted a woman this afternoon—I got you a woman. What's wrong with her?

ERNIE *plays the third ball.*

3   ERNIE. Yours is all right.

4   MICK. So what's wrong with yours?

5   ERNIE. Her ears are too big.

6   MICK. What you worrying about her ears for! You want to get a grip on yourself, son! I mean—let's face it—you're not Elvis Presley.

7   ERNIE. I'm not going, Mick—that's all.

8   MICK. Look—we're taking them to the pictures—you can watch the picture.

ERNIE *plays the fourth ball.*

9   ERNIE. What's on?

10   MICK. 'Time and Again.' It's funny.

11   ERNIE. I've seen it.

12   MICK. So we'll go to the Odeon.

13   ERNIE. I'm not lashing out two-and-nine on that big-eared bint.

14   MICK. All right. All right, Ernie—I'll tell you what. We'll swop over. After the news.

15   ERNIE. Straight up?

16   MICK. Dead level.

ERNIE *plays the fifth ball.*

17   ERNIE What time did you line them up for?

18   MICK. Two o'clock. On the dot. Outside the Pleasure Gardens. We'll have to shift before they do a bunk or get fixed up.

ERNIE *straightens his tie.*

19   ERNIE. No hurry, man. Take your time. They can wait.

ERNIE *and* MICK *stroll off, hands in pockets, towards the entrance of the arcade. As they pass the darts stall* LOMAX *calls out to them.*

1 LOMAX. Try the darts, lads? Sixty-five or over takes a prize!

MICK *replies without so much as a glance at* LOMAX.

2 MICK. Stick 'em.

MICK *and* ERNIE *move towards the main entrance and* LOMAX *turns away disconsolately. As* MICK *and* ERNIE *approach the doors a girl,* PENELOPE BELFORD, *enters the arcade.* MICK *turns to whistle at her but, receiving no encouragement, moves on and out with* ERNIE, *through the doors. The girl looks hesitantly around the arcade and then crosses to* LOMAX.

3 PENELOPE. Excuse me. . . .

LOMAX *swings round in the belief that he has found a customer. He attempts, unsuccessfully, to ape* FENTRILL'S *approach and mannerisms.*

4 LOMAX. Hello!

5 PENELOPE. I'm trying to get to . . .

6 LOMAX. You've come to the right place then. Come over here a minute. No, come on—come a bit closer.

7 PENELOPE [*hanging back*]. All I want to know is . . .

8 LOMAX. Never mind that for a minute, 'cause I'm going to do you a favour, missis woman. [*He points to the back of the stall.*] Now, you see what it says up there, don't you? It says sixty-five or over—and it's only a tanner for three darts—but you get fifty-five or over and you can have anything you like from the bottom shelf. Now just you . . .

PENELOPE *shakes her head—almost uncomprehending. During the above speech she has been backing slowly away from* LOMAX. *Now, she turns and crosses the arcade towards the rifle range.* LOMAX, *undeterred, jumps over the counter of the darts stall and moves quickly over to the rifle range as* PENELOPE *approaches. He uses the* MASON *technique—unsuccessfully.*

How about the rifles then? Only nineteen and you get a prize. All the guns are balanced and tested. Tanner—that's all.

PENELOPE veers away from the rifle range and again crosses the arcade approaching COPPIN. She stops, takes a wallet from her raincoat pocket, opens it and extracts an envelope. She stands, looking at the envelope, indecisively and almost distressed. CURTIS looks up at her and speaks gently.

2 CURTIS. You—looking for someone, miss?

PENELOPE looks up—not really comprehending.

I mean, is there something I can do, like?

3 PENELOPE. Thank you. [*She indicates the envelope*]. It's this. I'm trying to find an hotel. The Sea-View Hotel.

4 CURTIS. Is that all you've got? Just the name?

PENELOPE nods.

Sea-View. . . . Sea-View. . . . Now let me think a minute. I know the name. Yes, that's it! Dorville Road. You want a number seven bus. You'll get one on the foreshore.

5 PENELOPE. Number seven?

6 CURTIS. Then ask the conductor for Dorville Road. Anybody'll tell you then.

CURTIS hands back the envelope and PENELOPE replaces it in the wallet, returning the wallet to her pocket.

7 PENELOPE. Thanks. Thank you very much.

PENELOPE turns to leave.

8 CURTIS. No, wait on! Just a minute! How about a go on here then? Before you go? . . . Well, it's only a tanner. Eight winning numbers.

9 PENELOPE. All right.

PENELOPE takes a coin from her raincoat pocket and hands it to CURTIS. Quickly and haphazardly, she rolls the five balls down the table and turns to go.

146

1 CURTIS. Don't start rushing off, love. Got to count them up first. You never know what you might have won. Look here—you've got five and five's ten and three's thirteen and two two's are seventeen. Seventeen! That's a winning number! Whoops, Missis Worthington, your mother's won a duck! You're up, love.

PENELOPE *smiles—for the first time.* CURTIS *takes down a plaster statuette: 'The Crinoline Lady', or 'Alsatian', and hands it to* PENELOPE. *She takes the statuette in both hands, looks down at it and the smile fades from her face. For some reason she is puzzled. Suddenly she turns, still clasping the statuette, and hurries out of the arcade.* CURTIS *watches her go slightly bewildered.* COPPIN *crosses from the rear of the arcade and approaches* CURTIS.

2 COPPIN. What's up with her?

3 CURTIS [*shaking his head*]. Don't ask me?

COPPIN *moves on to* LOMAX *who has returned to the darts stall.*

4 COPPIN. All right, Harry?

5 LOMAX. Yeh—all right, Frank. What time you pushing off for lunch?

6 COPPIN. Two—should've been. Sailor's let me down again. He was due back quarter of an hour since.

LOMAX *swings himself over the counter.*

7 LOMAX. You get off if you want. I'll keep a skeg on the rifles. We won't do much today.

8 COPPIN. The silly old nit. One day the boss is going to stroll in and we'll have a joint going spare-handed. He'll cop it then.

9 LOMAX. Sailor don't worry.

10 COPPIN. Worry him if he gets the push.

11 LOMAX. It's the last day.

12 COPPIN. There's other years to think about.

13 LOMAX. Course—suppose there is. . . . But not for this kiddie —tonight it's curtains. Will I be glad to see the back of this place.

147

COPPIN moves away from the darts stall.

1 COPPIN. Yeh.... Look, if the old burk does come in—give us a shout, eh?

2 LOMAX. Right.

COPPIN crosses arcade and enters workshop. CURTIS leaves the marble alley and crosses to the darts stall.

3 CURTIS. You got a light, Harry?

LOMAX fishes a box of matches from his pocket and tosses them to CURTIS. CURTIS lights a cigarette behind the following dialogue and returns the box to LOMAX.

4 LOMAX. Sailor looks like dropping in for it.

5 CURTIS. One of these days he will. It gets towards the back end of the season and he stops caring, you know.

6 LOMAX. You got a job lined up for the winter, Tich?

7 CURTIS. Oh, I don't know. I think I'll just, sort of, knock around the town, Harry.

8 LOMAX. For six months!

9 CURTIS. It gets a habit, Harry.

10 LOMAX. I just don't understand you blokes.

11 CURTIS. Do it for a year or two and you get used to it.

12 LOMAX. So what do you live on?

13 CURTIS. Take things steady. Cut down on fags and that. Save a couple of pounds a week through the summer and with what I get from the Labour I manage.

14 LOMAX. Move off to the big towns, boy, and you could get a job easy.

15 CURTIS. Happen so.... I don't know.... You don't bother.

16 LOMAX. Sailor O.K.—and George and Jack—you can see their point—this is home for them. But you—you don't belong to these parts.

17 CURTIS. Almost. I've had twelve years of it.

18 LOMAX. So it's time you did a bunk. You could make a living.

1 CURTIS. I was a skilled tradesman. Painter and decorator.

2 LOMAX. There you are!

3 CURTIS. Went back to it after the war. Then we had the kiddie and the wife pegged it.

4 LOMAX. Bit of hard luck that, Tich.

5 CURTIS. Yes.

6 LOMAX. Where do you come from? Home, I mean?

7 CURTIS. Manchester. See, with the wife gone and me left with the kiddie it was hard going.

8 LOMAX. Boy?

9 CURTIS. Little lass. Well, you know, Sheila that's—that was the wife—she had a sister. In Bolton. So with me being on my own her sister says she'll look after it. The kiddie, see.

10 LOMAX. Make it easier for you.

11 CURTIS. And I didn't want to hang round home no longer. Not on my own, you know.

12 LOMAX. Yeh. I know.

13 CURTIS. So I got on a train—ended up here. Easter forty-six that was. The Governor set me on. In the summer, you know, you meet people on this job. You know—same people come holidaying year after year—you make friends.

14 LOMAX. You could set up a pitch in the big city—any of the big towns. You've got the kid growing up.

15 CURTIS. So after the season finished—first time—I went up to Bolton. The daughter was coming up for three. She didn't want to know—you know, was calling the wife's sister her mam. They wanted to bring her up that way—haven't got no kiddies of their own. I mean, they do pretty well—he manages a shop. She didn't know I was her dad. Better for her that way, I suppose. I mean—what am I? But. . . . I don't know—the kiddie meant a lot to me. I mean, when a man's got a kid he's . . . he's big, you know. Used to send me a card Christmas—on

my birthday sometimes. To Mr. Curtis. Dropped off the last two or three years.

2   LOMAX. You never see her?

CURTIS *shakes his head.*

3   CURTIS. Better for her if not. Must be fifteen—sixteen now. Used to reckon on going up again sometime. I'm a lousy eight quid a week six month a year grafter—that's not a lot to be. I've got a kid though, Harry.

4   LOMAX. You're all right, Tich.

5   CURTIS. I mean, I wanted to send them a couple of quid every week for the kiddie. They didn't want it.

6   LOMAX. If they won't take it it's not your fault, Tich.

7   CURTIS. I mean, so I'm a grafter, Harry. What's wrong with that?

8   LOMAX. It's a living—same as any other job.

9   CURTIS. You know what I've always said, Harry? One year I'm going up there and see that kid and the wife's sister can go to hell.

10 LOMAX. It's your kid, Tich.

11 CURTIS. So one year I'm going to go up there and see that kid. 'Look', I'm going to say, 'look, Mary, I'm a silly old nit—I'm an eight-quid-a-week-touch-grafter on a sea-side pitch scratching for tanners. I've never been no good to anybody but I'm your old man.'

12 LOMAX. You should do it.

13 CURTIS. When the kid was young I couldn't manage—not to keep a house going and a job and look after the kid as well. But now—now I could start up again, Harry.

14 LOMAX. Easy enough.

15 CURTIS. I'm a tradesman. I'm a skilled hand. I could get a job and a house all right.

16 LOMAX. So you don't want to know no more than that.

17 CURTIS. A twelve month a year job.

18 LOMAX. That's what you want.

1   CURTIS. I ought to do that, Harry.

2   LOMAX. What's the good of talking about it? Less of the patter. As soon as this joint folds you want to be on your way.

3   CURTIS. Yes—why not?

4   LOMAX. This year, Tich. Not keep on nattering. Just do it.

5   CURTIS. That's right.

6   LOMAX. That's your kid.

7   CURTIS. Are they in for a shock in Bolton! This year, Harry, I'm going to make a start all over again.

8   LOMAX. That's the way.

9   CURTIS. What about you? Are you stopping on?

10   LOMAX. Tomorrow morning I'm on the puffer.

11   CURTIS. Got a job to go to?

12   LOMAX. Not yet. I reckon I could get fixed up on lorries.

13   CURTIS. Lorries?

14   LOMAX. Long distance. Get a pitch as a driver's mate, first off. Cop on for my own truck later on. You know.

15   CURTIS. If you come up north any time you could call in and see us. Me and the nipper.

16   LOMAX. Course I will.

17   CURTIS. Have a cup of tea and that. Hey! That'd be a handy number for you, Harry. You'd see the country then all right.

18   LOMAX. If I could land a job like that.

19   CURTIS. Don't see why not, boy.

    SANDERS *enters through main entrance and approaches the darts stall.*

20   SANDERS. Afternoon, Tich, Harry.

21   CURTIS. Afternoon, Guv.

22   LOMAX. Afternoon.

    SANDERS *glances around the deserted arcade.*

23   SANDERS. Dropped off more than ever then?

1   LOMAX. Looks like it.

2   CURTIS. Might pick up a bit for the evening—last evening—Guv.

3   SANDERS. Done anything at all, have you?

4   LOMAX. Couple of bob, that's all.

SANDERS nods and notices the unattended rifle range.

5   SANDERS. Nobody on the guns?

6   LOMAX. Jack's away at his lunch.

7   CURTIS. Shouldn't be long now. Due back at a quarter past.

8   SANDERS. Who's supposed to be on relief?

LOMAX shrugs his shoulders—hesitant to involve BEESON.

9   LOMAX. Sailor . . . I suppose.

10 SANDERS. Not turned in yet?

11 CURTIS. Don't know. Haven't seen him, Guv.

SANDERS nods.

12 SANDERS. Frank about, is he?

13 LOMAX. He's in the back.

SANDERS nods again and then crosses and enters the workshop.

Sailor! The stupid decrepit old dick! He wants slinging. So what's he think he's playing at?

14 CURTIS. He's done it this time, Harry. He's had it coming for ages.

The record player is switched on again from the workshop and the speakers blare out a different tune. FENTRILL *enters through the main entrance and crosses to the darts stall.*

15 FENTRILL. Now then, my little lads. Been doing it all for me, then?

FENTRILL vaults over the counter, examines the box at rear of the stall and turns to LOMAX.

What's this then? What's up, like? Two bob? A stinking florin! A rotten dinar! What did you do—nip off to the Regal?

1   LOMAX. Been dead, George. Had nobody in.

    FENTRILL *turns to* CURTIS.

2   FENTRILL. And what have you got to make so much noise about?

3   CURTIS. It's Sailor. He's not turned in again.

    FENTRILL *glances across at the unattended rifle range.*

4   FENTRILL. Governor back yet, is he?

5   LOMAX. Just strolled in. He's in the back with Frank.

6   FENTRILL. Aaahh—so what. I should do my nut over the admiral. He's not with us half the time. Me—me with another mouth to feed and on the Old King Cole* tomorrow.

7   CURTIS. You heard any more about the wife, George?

8   FENTRILL. You think there's another still to come or something? What's all this—'heard any more' bull? Nip up tonight and once her over—that's all. Tap the Guv for a spare half hour at tea break.

    MASON *enters through the main entrance and crosses to the darts stall. He is wearing a raincoat and carries a rolled newspaper.*

    Here he is, Prince Honolulu, the bookies' bread and butter merchant. Down the course again, Jack?

9   MASON. George! They're up, boy! I've got the first two up in my treble.

10   CURTIS. You back a winner, Jack?

11   FENTRILL. Winner! He couldn't pick a winner in a one horse race. The day he picks a winner they'll disqualify it.

12   MASON. It's in the paper, George. I've just been in the bookies. The first two nags are past the post.

    FENTRILL *snatches the paper from* MASON, *glances at the back page, then screws up the paper and throws it on the floor.*

13   FENTRILL. It's a lousy misprint.

* = dole.

MASON *retrieves the paper and smooths the pages carefully.*

1 MASON. Here, steady on, George! I've told you, I've been in the bookie's. They've got it up on the board. This is it, boy. Two home and one to go.

2 LOMAX. What price did you get, Jack?

3 MASON. Dollar on a ten to one all on to a twenty to one.

4 FENTRILL. You what! [FENTRILL *snatches the paper and studies the back page.*]

5 MASON. In the stop press.

6 CURTIS. That's a lot of money, eh, Jack?

7 LOMAX. It's over fifty quid!

8 MASON. Easily. I haven't worked it out yet.

9 CURTIS. In the money, eh, Jack?

10 FENTRILL. It's near on seventy! Five bob on a ten to one gives you two-fifteen to come with your stake all on a twenty to one shot gives you sixty-eight fifteen plus your stake gives you seventy-one ten. Seventy-one nicker and half a bar!

11 MASON. All going on to the one in the two-thirty.

12 LOMAX. Seventy-one quid on the next race!

13 FENTRILL. Aaahh—you'll not get that. He'll pay on the limit. Sixty-six to one.

14 MASON. It's on with the big firm—no limit.

15 FENTRILL. There's got to be a limit.

16 MASON. There's no limit!

17 CURTIS. What have you got to come if the next one wins, Jack?

18 FENTRILL. Next one wins! Don't give me that. He's done his cash. The next one's going down the course. Nobody has it that good.

19 MASON. That's all you know. This one in the next has been backed down. Eight to one in the paper this morning—nine to four in the last shout. They've backed it right down.

1 LOMAX. Seventy quid on a nine to four shot!

2 MASON. It'll start off favourite.

3 FENTRILL. Seventy quid on the next fav!

4 MASON. It's a good thing.

5 LOMAX. It'll be over two hundred nicker if it comes up.

6 MASON. Backed down from eight to one to nine to four it's going to romp home.

7 FENTRILL. You jammy burk!

8 MASON. I told you this morning—you could have been in with me!

FENTRILL *takes a half-crown from his pocket and slaps it on the counter.*

9 FENTRILL. Here you are, Jack. Half a dollar for a half share.

MASON *flicks the coin off the counter and it falls behind the darts stall.*

10 MASON. Stick it.

11 FENTRILL. Go steady on!

FENTRILL *ducks down and retrieves the coin.*

Flinging my money about like a bloke with no arms.

12 MASON. You wait till the result of the two-thirty comes in, son. I'll be flinging my own about then. Years I've waited for a touch like this. Two hundred nicker! What! Crafty deposit on a little boarding house and Jack's in business. Seventeen and six a day B. and B. and ten guineas a week all found. Let the wife do the grafting.

13 FENTRILL. You wouldn't turn capitalist, Jack. Who's going to scrape the candy-floss off the glass next season? Who's going to see to the rifles?

14 MASON. You want me to tell you what you can do with the guns, George? Pellets, prizes, little cardboard targets and the lot.

15 CURTIS [*sings*]. Every time it rains it rains—pennies from Heaven.

1   FENTRILL. All right, Robeson,* you can jack that in.

   MASON *glances across at the unattended rifle range.*

2   MASON. Here, who's supposed to be on the guns, anyway?

3   LOMAX. What's your interest? I thought you'd retired?

4   MASON. I have. But I don't come into my inheritance until after the two-thirty.

5   CURTIS. Sailor's not back yet, Jack.

6   MASON. Not again. Twice he's been warned this week. If the Governor gets in first today . . .

   LOMAX *indicates the workshop.*

7   LOMAX. The Governor's got in first.

8   MASON. What? He's back? And I'm stood here chatting you blokes up?

   FENTRILL *vaults over the counter.*

9   FENTRILL. Got to make a start sometime, I suppose.

   SANDERS *and* COPPIN *come out of the workshop.*

10   SANDERS. You know how it is, Frank. I know how long he's been with the firm—he was here when I was a kid and the old man was handling. All the same, you can't put up with it for ever.

   SANDERS *glances up as* MASON *and* FENTRILL *pass him on their way into the workshop.*

   Afternoon, lads.

11   MASON. Afternoon, Guv. Frank.

12   FENTRILL. Going to do it all this afternoon, are we?

13   COPPIN. We hope so.

   MASON *and* FENTRILL *go into the workshop as* SANDERS *and* COPPIN *lean against the machines at the rear of the arcade.*

   I told him this morning—it's every time he goes out he's

   * Paul Robeson—famous popular singer.

late back. The other lads drop in for it. They have to work the extra to cover for him.

2 SANDERS. I don't know. . . . I'd better see him later on this afternoon.

3 COPPIN. I'll tell him when he comes in.

SANDERS nods and crosses to go into the office. MASON and FENTRILL enter from the workshop, shrugging on their uniform jackets as they cross to their respective stalls. COPPIN calls across to the darts stall.

Harry!

4 LOMAX. Coming.

FENTRILL swings himself over the counter of the darts stall as LOMAX leaves it to cross to COPPIN. Business is picking up slightly and three or four customers have come in through the main entrance and are wandering around the arcade. FENTRILL goes into his usual spiel and calls out to a WOMAN who is examining a slot machine. The record player blares in the background.

5 FENTRILL. Here we are then! Who says the jolly old darts! Hey, you! Missis Woman! Come here a minute. No, no, no! I don't want you to play darts. I want to show you something. Come over here!

The WOMAN approaches FENTRILL. The other attendants pick up their cues from FENTRILL and go into their respective spiels. LOMAX approaches COPPIN.

6 LOMAX. You want me, Frank?

COPPIN takes a small bag of loose change from his pocket and hands it to LOMAX.

7 COPPIN. You'd better cop on to the loose change until Sailor decides to call in and see us.

LOMAX empties the contents of the bag into his pocket.

8 LOMAX. Right. You reckon he's for the high jump? Get the push this time?

9 COPPIN. I shouldn't be at all surprised. The silly old crackpot.

1 LOMAX. Poor old Sailor. He'll have a job on finding another pitch at his age.

2 COPPIN. That's his worry. I've done my best.

3 LOMAX. Yeh.

> COPPIN *moves away, down centre of arcade, as* LOMAX *goes into his spiel.*

Change, any change or copper required! Get your change then! Change, any change!

> *The afternoon is passing and the arcade is busier than we have yet seen it. There are five or six customers wandering around the machines and stalls, the attendants are all shouting and the record player is at full volume. A* CUSTOMER *approaches* LOMAX *and hands him a shilling.*

4 CUSTOMER. Give us a bobsworth, Jack.

> LOMAX *counts out the change and hands it to the* CUSTOMER.

5 LOMAX. Three and three's six and three's nine and three's twelve.

6 CUSTOMER. Thanks.

> *The* CUSTOMER *pockets the coins and moves off down the arcade as* LOMAX *again goes into his spiel.*

7 LOMAX. Change, any change! Get your change then! Who wants change!

> *The attendants suddenly stop their respective spiels as* BEESON *enters through the main door. Though not drunk, he has obviously been drinking.* COPPIN *pauses and waits as* BEESON *approaches him.*

8 COPPIN. You stupid nit. You silly old burk!

9 BEESON. Afternoon, Frank.

> COPPIN *shakes his head and moves towards the entrance.* BEESON *crosses and approaches the rifle range where* MASON *calls out to him.*

10 MASON. Who was supposed to be on relief on the rifles then?

11 BEESON. Now then, Jack!

Business has again dropped off in the arcade and the few remaining customers drift out during the following dialogue.

1 MASON. You're a right one, you are!

2 BEESON. What's up?

3 MASON. Where were you for starter's orders?

4 BEESON. My watch stopped.

5 MASON. Don't give me that. Swilling them back—guzzling—that's where you've been.

6 BEESON. I only dropped in for the odd one.

7 MASON. And the rest. Half an hour over the odds. The joint going spare-handed when the Guv strolled in.

8 BEESON. The Guv?

9 MASON. He's in his office. Stamping your cards up.

10 BEESON. He wouldn't shop me, Jack.

11 MASON. You've shopped yourself.

12 BEESON. Go on—I've been here too long for that.

13 MASON. You'll not be here much longer.

14 BEESON. I was here when his father opened up first off.

COPPIN *approaches the rifle range.*

15 COPPIN. Sailor!

BEESON *turns.*

The Governor wants a word with you. Later on.

16 BEESON. It were just . . . I just lost count of the time, Frank.

17 COPPIN. Don't tell me. Have it out with the boss. You've had enough warnings and lettings off. . . . I'm sorry—it's not my fault.

COPPIN *moves off towards the workshop.*

18 BEESON. No. . . . Course not.

All the customers have now left the arcade. FENTRILL *vaults over the counter of the darts stall and crosses to the rifle range.* LOMAX *moves down the arcade to join the group at the rifle range.*

1 FENTRILL. How did you go on, then, Admiral? Has he given you the old front and back?

2 LOMAX. You got the push, Sailor?

3 BEESON. I was grafting for this firm when it started up.

4 FENTRILL. Well, you won't be here when it closes down, my old flower.

5 BEESON. On the end of the pier, that was, after the war. Not the last war, the one before that.

6 FENTRILL. The War of the Roses.

7 BEESON. Six machines the old man started off with. A rock and humbug joint on the end of the pier and half a dozen slot machines, and I was grafting for him then.

8 FENTRILL. So you've had a fair old crack of the whip.

9 BEESON. Five years spieling for the Headless Man and the Five Legged Pig.

10 FENTRILL. Barnum and Bailey never had a look in.

11 BEESON. I've been a showman all my life. In here.

12 FENTRILL. About time you jacked it in then.

13 BEESON. I never knew anything else.

14 FENTRILL. Aw—get knotted, you silly old burk.

> BEESON *goaded into a helpless fury by* FENTRILL, *also in fear and frustration, looks around for some means of releasing his emotions. He leans across the rifle range and picks up a very large plaster statuette of the 'Whistling Boy' or 'Girl with Alsations' variety.*

15 BEESON. The whole bloody joint wants wrecking!

> MASON *moves towards* BEESON *apprehensively.*

16 MASON. Go steady on, Sailor!

> MASON *is too late.* BEESON *raises the statuette above his head and smashes it down on the floor. For a moment there is complete silence and no one moves.* BEESON *stands looking down, in horror, now at the broken statuette.* COPPIN *enters from the workshop and crosses down the arcade towards the group at the rifle range. With the exception of* BEESON *the attendants break away and move off to their respective*

stalls as the door of the office opens and SANDERS *stands framed in the doorway.*

1 COPPIN. That's put the kybosh on it, Sailor. You stupid slob.

BEESON *continues to stare at the broken figure as* CURTIS *crosses from the marble alley carrying a shovel and a small hand-brush.* CURTIS *kneels and sweeps the pieces on to the shovel. He is singing to himself.*

2 CURTIS. Some died by the glenside and some 'mid the strangers,
And wise men have told us their cause was a failure.
But they fought for old Ireland and none have died braver,
Glory—Oh, Glory—Oh, to the bold Fenian men.

The lights fade.

SCENE 3   EVENING OF THE SAME DAY

It is eight forty-five and, with the exception of the employees, the arcade is again deserted. It is quite dark outside and the arcade is lit by strings of coloured lamps hanging above the stalls. The attendants are all standing by their respective stalls with the exception of FENTRILL *who has crossed to the rifle range where he is in conversation with* MASON. COPPIN *stands at the marble alley talking to* CURTIS. BEESON *stands in the centre of the arcade with a bag of small change and coppers slung round his neck.*

3 MASON. A short head. A rotten stinking short head!

4 FENTRILL. So what did you expect?

5 MASON. Seventy nicker on a nine to four shot all down the Swannee for the sake of a melt of a short head.

6 FENTRILL. You never stood a look in.

7 MASON. I could have been holding two hundred. I could have had it in my hand now.

8 FENTRILL. Boy, the day you swing a bet like that, boy—that will be the day.

1 MASON. I could have been all lined up for the boarding gaff next season. The bed and breakfast drum.

2 FENTRILL. I'll tell you where you'll be next season, my old china. Here. Grafting. Right here. With me—and him, and him, and him, and him.

During the above speech FENTRILL *points alternatively to* CURTIS, COPPIN, LOMAX *and* BEESON.

3 MASON [*as* FENTRILL *points to* BEESON]. Not him.

FENTRILL *shrugs his shoulders.*

4 FENTRILL. Nobody grafts for ever. . . . Come on, then. I'll give you a last go on the arrows before we lock up.

5 MASON. Tanner stakes?

6 FENTRILL. Make it a bob—I need the money. It's a long winter.

MASON *and* FENTRILL *cross over to the darts stall.* FENTRILL *takes a shilling from his pocket and tosses it.*

7 MASON. Heads.

FENTRILL *uncovers the coin.*

8 FENTRILL. You're away.

FENTRILL *places the coin on the counter.* MASON *takes a shilling from his pocket, places it beside* FENTRILL'S *coin and picks up three darts.*

9 MASON. Highest score with three arrows?

10 FENTRILL. When you're ready.

COPPIN *moves away from the marble alley and enters the office.* CURTIS *crosses down to watch the darts game as* FENTRILL *throws his first dart.*

11 CURTIS. Playing darts, George?

MASON *throws the second dart.*

12 FENTRILL. No, you soft twit, we're knitting a pullover. What does it look as if we're doing?

1 CURTIS. Playing darts, George?

2 FENTRILL. So belt up, will you?

3 CURTIS. Only trying to make a conversation, George.

MASON *throws his final dart.*

4 FENTRILL. Don't bother.

5 MASON. Sixty-four to beat.

FENTRILL *picks up three darts from the counter and raises his arm to throw the first one as* CURTIS *begins to sing to himself.*

6 CURTIS. Ching-ching Chinaman bought a penny doll,
Washed it, dressed it . . .

FENTRILL *turns.*

7 FENTRILL. Do we have to have that, then?

8 CURTIS. Sorry, George.

FENTRILL *throws the first dart as* BEESON *moves down the arcade to join the group.*

Tonight's the night, Jack. Tonight's the big night, boy.

9 MASON. What am I supposed to do? Handstands?

FENTRILL *throws the second dart.*

10 CURTIS. Out of work tomorrow, boy.

11 FENTRILL. You'll be out of teeth in a minute.

12 CURTIS. Sorry, George.

CURTIS *relapses into silence as* FENTRILL *throws the third dart.* FENTRILL *sighs, shakes his head, takes a shilling from his pocket and slams it on the counter.*

13 FENTRILL. Fifty-rotten-five.

MASON *picks up the coin.*

I'll end up on the pier flogging matches yet.

14 CURTIS. You lost, then, have you, like?

1 FENTRILL. No—it's his birthday.

2 CURTIS. It isn't, is it, Jack?

FENTRILL raises his hand in disgust and CURTIS skips out of reach. FENTRILL raises himself up to sit on the counter.

3 FENTRILL [*to* BEESON]. What you seeking, then, y'old melt?

4 BEESON. Nothing—nothing, George.

5 FENTRILL. You won't find it here.

6 CURTIS. You seen the Guv yet, Sailor? He had you in the office up to press?

BEESON shakes his head as LOMAX crosses down the arcade to join the group.

7 MASON. You'll be looking for a new fiddle next year, my old lad. After a different gaff.

8 FENTRILL. I can see him finding one.

9 BEESON. I'll get a pitch doing summat.

10 FENTRILL. What, for instance?

11 BEESON. I'll get a pitch.

12 FENTRILL. For instance?

13 BEESON. Must be something going somewhere.

14 FENTRILL. What?

15 BEESON. Must be lots of jobs on the go if you look for them.

16 FENTRILL. Just name me one. That's all. Just come across with one lumber a decrepit old dick like you could land!

17 MASON. Aw—leave him be, George.

18 BEESON. I'll get summat.

19 CURTIS. You keep on looking, Sailor. Something'll crop up.

20 BEESON. I could always go back to sea.

21 FENTRILL. You what!

22 BEESON. I could ship on.

23 FENTRILL. What as—a cabin boy.

1 BEESON. I could go back to fishing.

2 LOMAX. Deep sea, Sailor? You sailed on the trawlers, Sailor?

3 FENTRILL. Him? If he ever got into a bath he'd drown.

4 BEESON. I'll get a job. I'll find a pitch all right.

5 CURTIS. There's bound to be some jobs going. Sailor, There's always bound to be some sort of a job.

6 LOMAX. You want to try inland—get away from the water.

7 BEESON. I don't know rightly.

8 CURTIS. You haven't got the push from here yet, Sailor—happen the Guv might keep you on. Next season.

9 FENTRILL. What? With him coming in with a load on—clocking in all hours—then bashing up that handsome statuette—I can see that happening a mile off.

COPPIN *enters from the office and crosses down to join the group.*

10 CURTIS. You never know, George, he might happen keep him on.

There is an uneasy silence as COPPIN *approaches.*

11 COPPIN. You're wanted, Sailor. In the office.

12 BEESON. Yes. . . . Aye. . . . Right, Frank.

13 COPPIN. I shouldn't be stood standing about. I shouldn't keep him waiting.

BEESON *nods his head and moves off slowly towards the office. The members of the group turn and watch him go.* CURTIS *sings quietly.*

14 CURTIS. Farewell and adieu to you fair Spanish ladies,
Farewell and adieu to you ladies of Spain.
For we've received orders for to sail for old England,
And so shall we never see you again. . . .

BEESON *enters the office and the door closes behind him. A moment's pause.*

15 MASON. Is he giving him the push?

16 COPPIN. Don't ask me, I only work here. I'll say this much—he's not giving him a gold watch and chain.

1 LOMAX. Poor old Sailor.

2 FENTRILL. Aah, well, what's it matter, anyway? We'll all be signing on tomorrow.

3 MASON. Another year gone.

4 COPPIN. Roll on next season.

5 FENTRILL. That's it. That's it, boy. Roll on next holiday-time and let's have some bonus. Good weather and train-loads of trippers. Roll on next year. Let's get back to the hard graft.

6 COPPIN [indicating LOMAX]. We won't have me-laddo here with us then. He's getting out of it—aren't you, Harry?

7 LOMAX. First train out won't be too soon.

8 MASON. New lad next season. They come and go.

9 FENTRILL. What you got lined up then, Harry? Got a bird wants laying, have you.

10 LOMAX. Not sticking in this dump all the winter, that's for certain.

11 COPPIN. He's got some sense.

12 LOMAX. See me pulling out of that station tomorrow morn-ing, boy. On that chuffer. Whoo-whoo! Let me get out of it. That's all. Just let me get fixed up with a steady number—chuff this six month a year lark for a game of billiards.

13 FENTRILL. Which way are you floating?

14 LOMAX. Anyway. What's it matter? Anyway away from here. Farther north, happen. Tich is going that way as well.

FENTRILL turns and looks at CURTIS.

15 FENTRILL. Who? Him?

16 CURTIS. It was only just that I was thinking about it, Harry.

17 FENTRILL. The day he moves out of here he'll be carried out.

18 CURTIS. It was just something I was thinking over.

19 LOMAX. You're going, Tich, aren't you? I mean, you said you were going.

1 FENTRILL. He's on a life sentence.

2 CURTIS. Well, I'm thinking about it, Harry—it's a—sort of—well, it's a big decision to come to, all at once like that.

3 MASON. Where are you reckoning on blowing to, Tich?

4 FENTRILL. He's not going anywhere. Who's going to look after all them bloody marbles? Start of the season next year and we'll have old Caruso here half an hour before the joint opens—hammering on the doors to be let in.

5 CURTIS. Just that I've been turning it over in my mind, like.

6 LOMAX. You're going, though, aren't you, Tich?

7 CURTIS. Oh, I. . . . Well, I don't know. . . . Well—well, yes. I mean, leastways, I'm intending to. Well, that's what I want to do. . . . Sometimes. . . . Just that I thought I might wait a week, or two before I go—I mean, before I set off North. . . . Well, you never know, do you? I might get fixed up with a job in town here if I have a look round. . . . Well, what's the sense in moving on before I know whether I might be able to land a number here?

8 LOMAX. Here!

9 CURTIS. I might just drop in lucky.

10 LOMAX. Here! In the winter!

11 CURTIS. Some blokes get them. . . . I was talking to a chap last week. . . . So if I don't I can push off any time. I've got six months.

12 LOMAX. You won't make it.

13 CURTIS. It's only that I'm going to have a sort round first.

14 FENTRILL. Tell me the old, old story.

15 COPPIN [to CURTIS]. You'll be here—next year—you'll be here with the rest of us.

> FENTRILL *indicates the large teddy-bear which is on show among the prizes above the marble alley.*

16 FENTRILL. He wouldn't go away and leave that. He's been dusting that bloody bear so long he ought to have to marry it.

167

1 MASON. When are you going to get shut of that bear, Tich? Doesn't anybody ever win on your joint?

2 FENTRILL. You what! Win? On that carve-up? Score three million six thousand four hundred and eighty seven and you get a picture postcard of the north pier on Christmas Eve.

3 CURTIS. I get shut of some swag, George.

4 FENTRILL. Yeh—down your gullet. I've seen you gobbing that one-win chocolate when you thought nobody was watching you.

5 CURTIS. Not me, George.

6 FENTRILL. Fiddle, fiddle, fiddle.

7 CURTIS. I've never touched the swag, George.

8 FENTRILL. Don't give me the patter. You stand behind that gaff golloping sweeties till your eyes stick out like organ-stops. I wonder you can face your dinner.

9 CURTIS. You shouldn't say that, George.

10 FENTRILL [imitating him]. 'You shouldn't say that, George.' Get lost, you tiny twit. You've been tea-leafing* that swag as long as I can remember.

FENTRILL *levers himself down from the counter and turns away from* CURTIS *in disgust.* CURTIS *moves across and grasps* FENTRILL'S *sleeve in remonstration.*

11 CURTIS. You shouldn't say things like that, George. You didn't . . .

FENTRILL *swings round in a sudden burst of anger.*

12 FENTRILL. Get your rotten hands off me, you murk!

FENTRILL *pushes* CURTIS *away viciously and raises his fist. Before he can strike the first blow, however,* COPPIN *moves across and restrains him.*

13 COPPIN. That's enough.

14 FENTRILL. I'll put his teeth . . .

* = thieving.

168

1 COPPIN. I said, drop it!

> FENTRILL *hesitates and then drops his fist.* COPPIN *releases him.*

> All right, so we're all on the loose tomorrow—it's not his fault.

> FENTRILL *is about to apologize to* CURTIS *but, at a loss for words, he does it by way of a gesture.*

2 CURTIS. It's all right, George. S'all right, boy.

> FENTRILL *hesitates.*

3 FENTRILL. Forget it, Tich. Just forget it, eh?

4 MASON [*to* FENTRILL]. Come on, I'll chase you round the board for a florin.

5 FENTRILL. Fetch the arrows—you're off.

> MASON *climbs over the counter to retrieve the darts as the office door opens and* BEESON *enters the arcade.* LOMAX *is the first to notice* BEESON'S *return.*

6 LOMAX. Hey!

> *The members of the group turn as* BEESON *approaches, crossing down the arcade and joining the group who cluster around him.*

7 MASON. So?

8 BEESON. I'm stopping on.

9 CURTIS. Stopping, Sailor?

10 BEESON. Coming back next season. He's let me off.

11 CURTIS. I told you it'd be all right. He's all right, the Guv, you see.

12 FENTRILL. You haven't got the push then?

> BEESON *shakes his head.*

13 MASON. They can't sack Sailor—he comes with the fixtures and fittings.

14 FENTRILL. You mean to say we've got to put up with you for another season? [BEESON *nods.*] Well, you dirty old devil!

There'll be more tea spilt along the prom next summer than we'll ever get supped.

2 COPPIN. You want to behave yourself next year, Sailor. No more bother.

3 FENTRILL. He might die before then—there's always that to hope for.

4 MASON. Another annual reunion next Whit.

The group moves in on BEESON *to congratulate him as the office door opens and* SANDERS *enters the arcade. He moves down towards the group carrying wage packets and insurance cards. The men are silent.* SANDERS *approaches, stops—pauses before he speaks.*

5 SANDERS. Might as well call it a day, lads—we're only wasting the electric. Make an early night of it for once. Leave your takings in the office before you blow and if you drop your jackets in the back I'll get them off to the laundry. I'm . . . I'm sorry we haven't been able to stretch it another week but—well, but you know how it's been. Jack, that's yours.

SANDERS *hands a wage packet and insurance card to* MASON.

6 MASON. Thanks, Guv.

7 SANDERS. There's your bonus inside as well.

8 MASON. Right. Thanks.

9 SANDERS. Keep you going for a week or two, at any rate. And . . . and so I'll look forward to seeing you next season.

10 MASON. I'll be ready for the off.

They shake hands. MASON *moves away behind, crosses to the rifle range, picks up the box containing the day's takings, crosses to the office, where he leaves the box and then goes into the workshop.*

11 SANDERS. Sailor.

SANDERS *hands* BEESON *a wage packet and card.*

12 BEESON. Ta, Guv.

1 SANDERS. Don't go mad with that bonus this year. Spread it
out a bit—remember what I've said. [BEESON *nods.*] And
look after yourself over the winter.

They shake hands. BEESON *turns to move away and then turns back.*

2 BEESON. About the jacket, Guv. . . . I didn't bring a coat with
me this morning.

3 SANDERS. You'd better hang on to that, then. Drop it into
the house sometime. It'll be all right.

BEESON *nods and moves away behind. He crosses to the office where
he leaves the bag of loose change and then goes into the workshop.*

George—that's yours.

SANDERS *hands* FENTRILL *a wage packet and card.*

4 FENTRILL. Right.

5 SANDERS. The wife's had the nipper then? Frank was saying.

6 FENTRILL. Aye. Little lad.

7 SANDERS. Picked a right time of year to have it. End of the
season.

8 FENTRILL. We'll manage—I suppose. Have to.

9 SANDERS. Yes. . . . If there's anything at all. . . . You know,
like, anything you're wanting—you know where the
house is.

10 FENTRILL. We'll be all right.

11 SANDERS. If I'd have known earlier on I could have called in
at a shop—present sort of thing.

12 FENTRILL. You'd no need to bother.

SANDERS's *glance falls upon a large teddy bear above the marble alley.*

13 SANDERS. How about that for a start?

COPPIN, LOMAX, FENTRILL *and* CURTIS *look up at the bear.*

14 FENTRILL. Get shut of that and Tich'll be heart-broken.

15 SANDERS. Let's be having it down then, Tich.

CURTIS *looks solemnly around the group then, slowly, climbs on to the marble alley and takes down the teddy bear. The bear squeaks as his hands grasp it around the middle.*

1   CURTIS. I never knew it did that! I've had it stuck up on this joint for seven summers and I never knew it did that!

CURTIS *throws the bear to* FENTRILL *and climbs down from the stall.*

2   FENTRILL. Thanks, Guv. She'll like that—the wife—I mean the kid's a bit young for it yet but it'll come in handy in a few months' time, will this.

3   SANDERS. Get you something proper for it when I think on—call in and see you when the missis is out of dock and getting about a bit.

4   FENTRILL. Any time.

They shake hands.

5   SANDERS. So I'll be seeing you before next season whatever crops up.

FENTRILL *nods. He turns and collects his takings box from behind the darts stall and moves off to leave the box in the office before going into the workshop.* SANDERS *hands a wage packet and card to* CURTIS.

That's yours, Tich.

6   CURTIS. Yes, Guv—right, Guv.

7   SANDERS. We'll be seeing you again next year, I expect?

CURTIS *gives* LOMAX *an embarrassed glance before answering.*

8   CURTIS. Yes, Guv . . . I expect so.

SANDERS *nods as* CURTIS *moves away to collect his box from behind the marble alley and crosses to the office and then the workshop.* SANDERS *hands a wage packet and card to* LOMAX.

9   SANDERS. And yours, young man.

10   LOMAX. Ta. Thanks very much.

11   SANDERS. You know about the bonus?

1   LOMAX. Well, I've heard the lads talking.

2   SANDERS. You'll find it in with your wages—so you'll know what it is. So you won't come back saying I've given you too much.

3   LOMAX. No—no, I shan't do that.

They laugh—almost embarrassedly.

4   SANDERS. Frank tells me you're moving on?

5   LOMAX. I thought I'd have a look round—get fixed up with a job in the north. There's more jobs going that way than here.

6   SANDERS Nothing at all round here in the winter.

7   LOMAX. No. So they reckon.

8   SANDERS. Any road, if you do happen to find yourself stuck here next summer—we'll always be glad to set you on.

9   LOMAX. Thanks.

10   COPPIN. You getting the train in the morning, Harry? First off?

11   LOMAX. That's what I was thinking of doing.

12   COPPIN. Best way.

13   LOMAX. Only . . . well, I've got a bit of money saved up—I mean it might be an idea to hang on here for a day or two—have a bit of a holiday myself. Been watching other people have theirs all summer, so why not?

14   COPPIN. It's up to you.

15   SANDERS. Why not?

LOMAX *glances down at the insurance card in his hand.*

16   LOMAX. You never know—I might just cop on to a job while I'm hanging round.

17   COPPIN. Here?

18   LOMAX. I'm not counting on it or anything like that. Couple of days and I'm floating, don't you worry about that. Just that—well—there's no need to go dashing off like mad.

1 SANDERS. Suit yourself.

2 LOMAX. Yeh.

3 SANDERS. And, like I say, if you are around when we open—
drop in.

They shake hands.

4 LOMAX. Course.

LOMAX turns and moves off to the workshop.

5 COPPIN. It's a six to four on shot that lad'll be signing on at
the Labour on Monday.

6 SANDERS. He's a good lad. We could do with him next season.

7 COPPIN. Aye—I suppose we could.

SANDERS hands COPPIN the final packet and card.

8 SANDERS. Frank.

*COPPIN takes his wages and insurance card and puts them into the
pocket of his overall.*

9 COPPIN. Thanks, Bob.

10 SANDERS. So that's it. The end of another summer.

11 COPPIN. Soon be getting ready for the next. Things don't
alter—much.

12 SANDERS. No. Once every year you pay off half a dozen blokes
and every time you can't stand the sight of yourself.

13 COPPIN. Somebody has to do it.

*The workshop door opens and FENTRILL, MASON, CURTIS, BEESON
and LOMAX enter the arcade, having changed into the clothing they
wore on arrival. SANDERS and COPPIN watch the group as they move
down the arcade towards the entrance.*

14 CURTIS. Good night, Guv. G'night, Frank!

Ad libbed 'good nights' from the rest of the group.

15 SANDERS. Good night, lads!

16 COPPIN. Good night!

The group move off and go out through the front doors.

1 SANDERS. So why do they do it, Frank.

2 COPPIN. Why do any of us do it?

SANDERS *shakes his head.*

It's the tripper trade—that's all. And we're in it. We love it—let's face it. August, July, the start of September, the gaff's stashed full of screaming bints and spewing kids and we love it. You've got your pockets full of gelt— you're holding—the mugs are handing over loot as fast as you can coin it in so you stand behind a joint with a mouthful of patter and a great big grin. For two months of the year you're Barnum and Bailey rolled into one in a joint full of mugs. For two months of the year. . . . Bring a coat with you, did you?

3 SANDERS. I didn't bother.

4 COPPIN. You could have done with one tonight. The summer's over. I'll switch off and get mine. Are you cashing up?

5 SANDERS. No. I'll come round in the morning.

6 COPPIN. Yeh . . . Shan't be a minute.

COPPIN *crosses and goes into workshop.* SANDERS *moves across to the darts stall, picks up a set of darts and tosses them into a dart-board. One by one the lights in the arcade go out as they are switched off from the workshop. Finally, one single light remains—a dim unshaded lamp hanging by the entrance and controlled by a switch by the entrance door.* COPPIN *enters from the workshop shrugging on his coat. He crosses to* SANDERS.

Right?

7 SANDERS. When you're ready.

SANDERS *and* COPPIN *cross to the entrance where* COPPIN *bolts the first door and switches off the final light.* SANDERS *takes a last look around the arcade.*

O.K.?

1 COPPIN. O.K.

> SANDERS *and* COPPIN *go out and close the door behind them. We see them through the plate glass as* COPPIN *locks the door and hands the key to* SANDERS. *In the distance we hear* CURTIS *singing as he goes down the promenade. There is the sound of the sea.*

2 CURTIS. We'll rant and we'll roar, like true British sailors,
   We'll rant and we'll roar, like true sailormen.
   For we've received orders for to sail for old England,
   And so shall we never see you again . . .

> *The song dies away, drowned by the swell of the sea as the* CURTAIN FALLS.

Topics for Discussion

THE WAKE

1   What impression of Judy's character do we get from the first scene?

2   Does it seem that Terry is telling the truth about Joey in his long speech (*page 9, speech 5*)?

3   Which of the brothers do we feel most sympathy for in the end, and why?

DOUBLE, DOUBLE

4   This play was first written for students in such a way that each could act two contrasting roles. Do you see any *dramatic* advantages that the author has gained from this arrangement?

5   Is this play just written for laughs, or do you think the author has any ideas behind it?

6   Is Lillian right in her attack on page 49 (*speech 6*)?

7   If you were producing this play, how much emphasis would you put on designing a fully realistic bus canteen for the scenery?

NO WHY

8   What different methods of persuasion are used on Jacob?

9   Which of the relatives seems to you the least pleasant? Explain your reasons for the choice.

10   The play ends with the stage direction: 'He waits, as if for a word. Do any of us speak? No. And if we did, what would we say?' What does the author mean?

11   What is the point of the title?

SEE THE PRETTY LIGHTS

12   What does Norman feel about his actual life, as far as we can tell from the speech on page 97 (*speech 1*)?

13   Norman's speech to Enid is rather similar to one of Gimlet's in *Double, Double* (*page 57, speech 3*). Are there any similarities in the two men? Do they feel bitter about their work?

14   Enid asks Norman (*page 99, speech 8*) why he isn't married. What seems to you to be the full reason?

15   Do you feel sorry for these two, or are they just foolish?

16   If you were producing this, would you expect the audience to laugh much? In which places? How should the actors play those parts?

LAST DAY IN DREAMLAND

17   What does the owner, Sanders, feel about the business?

18   'You what! Win? On that carve-up? Score three million six thousand four hundred and eighty-seven and you get a picture postcard of the north pier on Christmas Eve' (*page 168, speech 2*). This is one of Fentill's many attacks. Is he serious? What sort of a person is he?

19   Does it seem likely that Lomas will in fact be back next year?

20   'So one day, before you know where you are, you're fifty-two and all you've got is a screwdriver, a fistful of loose change and sixth months' work a year' (*page 134, speech 4*). Are these men drifters? Do they like this life? Or is it unavoidable for them?

21   If you had to shorten the play, do you consider the section with Penelope (*pages 145–7*) could be cut, or would anything important to the play as a whole be lost if that were cut?

22   Is this play meant just as a realistic picture of life in an amusement arcade? If not, why has the author chosen this setting?

The Authors and their Work

Including recommendation of other plays by
the same authors for reading in schools.

ALUN OWEN

A Welshman who spoke Welsh until he went to school, Alun Owen was born in 1926 and eight years later his parents moved to Liverpool—the setting of many of his plays. He said later: 'Liverpool and Wales, they're the two things I really know, and yet I'm not completely at home in either', and this estrangement comes up in this and many of his other plays. From school he went to do two years' war service as a miner. Stuck for a job after the war, he got work in a repertory theatre almost by chance. For the best part of twelve years after that he worked as an actor, including spells as a feed to a music hall comedian, and even as a dame in Pantomine.

Alun Owen has been writing since he was thirteen or fourteen. Of his first produced play, he said: 'Suddenly I wanted to write just a little episode—one event which came to me—as a drama, so I wrote *Two Sons* and sent it to the BBC. They produced it on the third programme, and I wrote another and another.'

Since then he has written a varied and constant stream of plays for the stage and television (forty at the time of writing), including a musical (*Maggie May*), a film (the Beatles' *A Hard Day's Night*), and even television comedy shows (the *Ronnie Barker Show* had three scripts by him). His special contribution to television has been recognized by three awards.

RECOMMENDED PLAYS

The Rough and Ready Lot (Encore Publishers)
Progress to the Park (Penguin *New English Dramatists 5*)
Three Television Plays (Cape)
Shelter (One act—Samuel French)

JAMES SAUNDERS

Of the playwrights represented in this volume, James Saunders is the only one who reflects the influence of the French dramatist Ionesco and the type of play which, because of its apparently lunatic dialogue and improbable events, is called 'the theatre of the absurd'. James Saunders came to writing late in life. A Londoner, born in Islington in 1925, he took a degree in chemistry, and became a teacher. It is said that his interest in playwriting started with the writing of snatches of dialogue, and certainly all his plays fascinate by their sequences of words. Later he was helped by a year's bursary for playwriting given by the Arts Council. His first work was produced on the radio, and then *Alas, Poor Fred* was produced in 1959 by a now famous theatre-in-the-round company in Scarborough. (It is interesting to compare David Campton's career and influence: see *Laughter and Fear* in this series.) In this, as in some of his other plays, violence is masked in the clichés of conventional chat. In *Barnstable*, for instance, the character of the title is not seen, but in a large gracious house full of standard characters using standard phrases about standard subjects we gradually discover that the building is falling down, unnoticed.

His two best-known full-length plays are *Next Time I'll Sing to You*, a puzzling and complex investigation of the purpose of life, and the slighter, *A Scent of Flowers*.

RECOMMENDED PLAYS

Barnstable (In *New Directions*, Hutchinson)
Next Time I'll Sing to You (Heinemann *Hereford Plays*)
A Scent of Flowers (Heineman *Hereford Plays*)
Neighbours and other Plays (Heinemann)

JOHN WHITING

When he was alive John Whiting achieved a reputation amongst some critics for the power, intelligence, and personal qualities of his plays. Since his early death in 1963 (at the age of forty-five) this reputation has been strengthened as his earlier plays have been revived and looked at afresh.

He was educated at Taunton School, and afterwards trained as an actor at the Royal Academy of Dramatic Art. For two years he worked in repertory, and then was in the army from 1939 until 1945. After the war he spent four years acting at Harrogate and York before he started to write plays. He has said: 'When I began writing, because I was miserably unsure of what I was doing, I used to make a dozen drafts. I am a totally uneducated person, with no academic education at all . . . well, I was at a public school, but I never passed an exam, and I didn't go to University. This shows some times.'

While he was acting he wrote various things, including an unpublished book about the war. His first play he thought did not work out well (though he later re-wrote it for television as *A Walk in the Desert*), but a remark by a friend who had read the book prompted him to try another one. This was *Saint's Day*. He did not expect anyone to produce it, but his third play, the whimsical comedy set in the Napoleonic Wars, *A Penny for a Song*, was produced in 1951— though it was not a success until a 1962 revival. Then *Saint's Day*, which Whiting had entered for a competition during that year of the Festival of Britain, was given an award, despite baffled dislike by the newspaper critics. The enthusiastic support from theatre people, who wrote of it as 'remarkable' in letters to the press, created a real battle between the objectors and those who liked it. The play does not seem as difficult now as it did then; it shows an old writer, a satirist, who has long withdrawn from the world, and is now obsessed with fears of violence. The play moves on to a dramatic series of violent events, and the self-destruction of the central character. It poses questions of responsibility for violence and tragedy as the central problem of our age.

John Whiting went on acting; his *Marching Song* was produced, with little success, in 1954. This play is now much admired: it shows the ex-General of a defeated European state faced with the choice of suicide or public trial and disgrace for his part in a military defeat. His next play, *The Gates of Summer,* closed whilst still on tour, before even reaching London. He then spent most of his time writing film scripts, until the Royal Shakespeare Company (now directed by Peter Hall, who as a Cambridge undergraduate had been much impressed by *Saint's Day*) actually commissioned him in 1961 to adapt a book about accusations of witchcraft amongst a mediaeval community of nuns. This play, *The Devils,* was really Whiting's first full public success, and has since been filmed. *No Why* was also performed by the Royal Shakespeare Company—two years after the author's death.

In many ways Whiting, represented here by the last of his plays, was the first of the fifties revival of a *writers'* theatre. We do not know what sort of plays he would have gone on to write, but we do know that he differed from the better known writers of the sixties (especially Arnold Wesker) in that he saw no place in drama for direct political and social pleading: his plays were written because he felt the need to write and make works of art—largely to express his feelings and please himself.

Readers who would like to know more about John Whiting will find the following helpful:

John Whiting by Ronald Hayman (Heinemann *Contemporary Play-wright* series).

An interview with Tom Milne and Clive Goodwin appears in *Theatre at Work,* edited by Charles Marowitz and Simon Trussler (Methuen).

RECOMMENDED PLAYS

All John Whiting's plays can be read in a two-volume collected edition, edited by Ronald Hayman (Heinemann).

Students are especially recommended the following, which are also available in single editions as noted:

Penny for a Song (Heinemann *Hereford Plays*)
Saint's Day (Heinemann *Hereford Plays*)
The Devils (Penguin *New English Dramatists 5*)

ALAN PLATER

Alan Plater started to write whilst still in his teens. He was born in Jarrow-on-Tyne, but his family moved to Hull when he was three. When he left Kingston High School, Hull, he went to King's College, Newcastle, to study architecture, which he saw, as he put it, as a 'respectable alternative to ivory towers'. After two years in an architect's office in Hull ('the only real job I've ever had'), he became a full-time writer when his first play, *The Smoke Zone,* was broadcast on the radio in 1961.

Sound radio gave him his first opportunities, and eight of his plays have been produced, including *The Mating Season.* Alan Plater has written an even larger number of plays for television, including *A Smashing Day, So-Long Charlie,* and *The Nutter.* The Z Cars series has been of especial interest to him, and one for which he has written eighteen scripts, as well as many of the best *Softly, Softly* scripts. He has also written a number of film scripts, including that for the film of D. H. Lawrence's *The Virgin and the Gypsy.*

The live theatre, particularly when closely attached to a particular region, interests Alan Plater most. The Victoria Theatre, Stoke-on-Trent has produced many of his stage plays, including *Ted's Cathedral.* This theatre has grown out of *local* interest, and Alan Plater feels strongly that the arts flourish most valuably in a regional setting so that each region needs an Arts Centre. He is deeply involved in schemes for such a centre in his own city, Hull. His latest plays have been the very successful musical *Close the Coalhouse Door, And a Little Love Besides,* and *Simon Said.*

OTHER RECOMMENDED PLAYS

A Quiet Night (in Z Cars, Longman)
Excursion (in *Playbill,* Hutchinson)
Mating Season (in *Worth a Hearing,* Blackie)
Close the Coalhouse Door (Methuen)

WILLIS HALL

Willis Hall was born in Leeds in 1929. His first opportunities for having his writing performed came when he was doing his military service in Malaya. There he wrote many scripts for the Chinese Schools Department of Radio Malaya. When he returned to England he started work as a journalist, but soon devoted all his time to playwriting, particularly for radio and television. His radio work included scripts for young listeners, and one serial, *The Royal Astrologers,* he later adapted for school performance (available in the *Kingswood Plays* series, published by Heinemann). A later play for young children, *The Gentle Knight,* has been published by Blackie. Television stimulated his writing of a large number of successful plays.

It was commission from an amateur group of actors from Oxford University that led to one of his most interesting and moving plays: *The Long and the Short and the Tall.* This shows a miscellaneous group of soldiers in the Malayan jungle during the Japanese advance on Singapore in 1942. They are faced with an acute problem: should they kill their Japanese prisoner to help their flight from the enemy? Cooped up in a deserted jungle hut, the strain of the situation reveals to us unexpected sides to their characters.

In 1960 he started a series of collaborations with his friend Keith Waterhouse (also born in Leeds in 1929). Together they adapted Keith Waterhouse's comic novel *Billy Liar* and have written plays, television scripts, and films (including *Whistle Down the Wind, Billy Liar,* and *A Kind of Loving*).

OTHER RECOMMENDED PLAYS

Air Mail from Cyprus a television play in *The Television Playwright* (Michael Joseph)

WITH KEITH WATERHOUSE

The Long and the Short and the Tall (Heinemann *Hereford Plays*)
Celebration (Evans)
Billy Liar (Blackie *Student Drama* series)

RECENT BRITISH DRAMA—*a reading list*

The five plays in this volume can serve as a taster for British Drama of the present time. The following list is a very limited choice of more plays to read from the very rich selection available. (I have prepared a wider list in *Towards the New Fifth*, Longman, 1969.) This list does not include the plays already recommended under each of the authors in this collection.

A helpful general survey for older readers is *Anger and After* by John Russell Taylor (Penguin and Methuen) and for sixth-form students the Heinemann *Contemporary Playwright* series is interesting and helpful. Each of these short books by Ronald Hayman discusses the works of one writer.

ARDEN, JOHN *The Business of Good Government* (Methuen *Modern Plays*)
  Sergeant Musgrave's Dance (Methuen *Modern Plays*)

BEHAN, BRENDAN *The Quare Fellow* (Faber)

BERMANGE, BARRY *No Quarter* (Methuen *Modern Plays*)

BOLT, ROBERT *A Man for All Seasons* (Heinemann *Hereford Plays*)

BRADLEY, ALFRED (editor) *Worth a Hearing* (Blackie *Student Drama* series)

CAMPTON, DAVID *Laughter and Fear*—nine one-act plays (Blackie *Student Drama* series)

CREGAN, DAVID *Three Men for Culverton* (Methuen *Playscripts*)

CROSS, BEVERLEY *One More River* (Rupert Hart-Davis)

DELANEY, SHELAGH *A Taste of Honey* (Methuen *Modern Plays*)

DURBAND, ALAN (editor) *New Directions* (Hutchinson)
  Playbill, three volumes of short plays (Hutchinson)

ENGLAND, BARRY *Conduct Unbecoming* (Heinemann *Hereford Plays*)

GALTON, RAY and SIMPSON, ALAN *Steptoe and Son* (edited by David Grant, Longman)

GOSLING, ALAN *A Dead Liberty* (Evans Plays)

JELLICOE, ANN *The Knack* (Faber)

LIVINGS, HENRY *Nil Carborundum* (Penguin *New English Dramatists*)

MARLAND, MICHAEL (editor) *Conflicting Generations,* television plays by Paddy Chayefsky, Ronald Eyre, John Hopkins, John Mortimer, and David Turner (Longman)
Six Scripts from 'Scene', television plays by Keith Dewhurst, Ronald Eyre, and Bill Lyons (Longman)
Z Cars, scripts from the television series by Keith Dewhurst, Ronald Eyre, John Hopkins, and Alan Plater (Longman)

OSBORNE, JOHN *Look Back in Anger* (Faber)
The Entertainer (Faber)

PINTER, HAROLD *The Birthday Party* (Methuen *Modern Plays*)
The Caretaker (Methuen *Modern Plays*)
Trouble in the Works (in *The Experience of Work*, Longman)

RECKFORD, BARRY *Skyvers* (Penguin *New English Dramatists*)

SCHAFFER, PETER *The Private Ear, The Public Eye* (Cape)
The Royal Hunt of the Sun (Longman)

SIMPSON, N. F. *The Hole*—2 sketches *One to Another* (Faber)
One Way Pendulum (Faber)

SPEIGHT, JOHNNY *If There Weren't Any Blacks You'd Have to Invent Them* (Methuen *Playscripts*)

STOREY, DAVID *The Contractor* (Cape)
Home (Cape)

TERSON, PETER *Zigger-Zagger* (Penguin)

WESKER, ARNOLD *Chips With Everything* (Blackie *Student Drama* series
The Kitchen (Penguin *New English Dramatists 2*)
The Trilogy (Longman)